KASHMIR SHAIVISM

The Secret Supreme

KASHMIR SHAIVISM

The Secret Supreme

Revealed by

SWAMI LAKSHMANJOO

edited by John Hughes

Lakshmanjoo Academy

Published by:

Lakshmanjoo Academy

First printing 1985
Second printing 1988 (revised)
Third printing 2000 (revised)

Printed in the United States of America

For information,
Lakshmanjoo Academy
http://www.lakshmanjooacademy.org

ISBN 978-0-9837833-3-6 (paperback)
ISBN 978-0-9837833-6-7 (hardcover)

The Book

This book, *Kashmir Shaivism: the Secret Supreme*, by the century's great philosopher saint Swami Lakshmanjoo, presents a systematic unfolding of the Tantric teachings of the ancient tradition of Kashmir Shaivism. This profound tradition, long enshrouded in secrecy, is so rich and detailed in its descriptions of what it reveals as the ascent of individual consciousness to universal God consciousness that it has been characterized as a mystical geography of awareness. Within the pages of this book is found the key of the oral tradition which unlocks its secrets and provides the reader with the tools necessary to venture into this wondrous landscape.

KASHMIR SHAIVISM “The Secret Supreme”

GUIDE TO PRONUNCIATION

The following English words exemplify the pronunciation of selected Sanskṛit vowels and consonants. The Romanized Sanskṛit vowel or consonant is first listed and then a English word is given to aid you in its proper pronunciation.

a	as	a in **A**merica.
ā	as	a in f**a**ther.
i	as	i in f**i**ll, l**i**ly.
ī	as	i in pol**i**ce.
u	as	u in f**u**ll.
ū	as	u in r**u**de.
ṛi	as	ri in mer**ri**ly.
ṛī	as	ri in ma**ri**ne.
e	as	e in pr**e**y.
ai	as	ai in **ai**sle.
o	as	o in st**o**ne.
au	as	ou in h**ou**se
ś	as	s in **s**ure
ṣ	as	s in **sh**un , bu**sh**
s	as	s in **s**aint, **s**in

TABLE OF CONTENTS

Preface to the Fourth Edition

Kashmir Shaivism: The Secret Supreme was first published in 1985. In 1988, a second edition was brought out which corrected numerous spelling errors and printing inconsistencies present in the first edition. In 2000, the third edition was brought out. In this edition a number of corrections and alterations were made for the sake of greater clarity. In addition the grammar was revised and an extensive index was added to facilitate easy reference. The present volume is the fourth edition and the fourth printing of this book. In this edition a final careful scrutiny was undertaken which resulted in a few corrections and alterations and clarifications. It is felt by one and all that this is the last time this text will need to be edited and or corrected.

John Hughes

Preface to the First Edition

This book consists of lectures that I delivered in 1971–1972. It began in 1969 when Maharṣi Mahesh Yogī came to our Valley. He had heard of me and wanted us to meet so he called on me. When he visited me, he asked if I would speak to his disciples and I agreed. He sent his transport and I was taken to where he was staying with his Western disciples. When I arrived, there was a huge gathering of Western devotees waiting for me. I spoke to them, giving a discourse on important points in Kashmir Śaivism.

John and Denise Hughes were also present at that gathering, but at that time I had not yet met them. They must have been impressed with what they heard for, in 1971, they returned to Kashmir and came to see me at my Āshram. I asked them who they were. They said they were Maharṣi's disciples. They explained to me that they had heard my discourse when they first came to Kashmir with Maharṣi in 1969. John then told me that he had one problem: he wanted to learn Kashmir Śaivism and would I have time to teach him? I replied, "Yes, I have enough time." I instructed him that he should come to the Āshram on the next Tuesday and I would begin teaching him. So on Tuesday he arrived, along with his tape recorder, and I began giving him lectures in the Āshram hall. Denise, his wife, also attended these lectures.

In the beginning, I taught John only the introductory topics of Kashmir Śaivism. As time passed, however, I came to know that John had good power of understanding and I became fond of him. I wanted to tell him more and more about Kashmir Śaivism, to teach him Śaivism's secrets, so I continued giving lectures and John recorded them. This was the main starting point of his studies. It is these secrets, these major points which I taught him at that time, which comprise this book.

As I appreciated that John was assimilating the lectures very well, after they were completed I started teaching him the theory which is found in the Śaiva scriptures. In this manner, Kashmir Śaivism was taught to him.

I think, when these lectures are printed, it will be a great boon for mankind and will elevate the whole world. Also, I will consider myself blessed by Lord Śiva. I hope that John will continue writing on what I have delivered to him in theory and practice — the Secrets Supreme. If he continues to expose it to the world, it will be a great help for everyone.

Swami Lakshmanjoo
1984

Introduction to the Third Edition

On the 27th of September 1991, the fully realized saint, beloved teacher and spiritual guide Swami Lakshmanjoo departed from this mortal world. As I mentioned in my earlier introduction to the present volume, it was Swamiji's fervent desire that the teachings and knowledge of Kashmir Śaivism be preserved long after his passing from this world. It was my great fortune to be able to audio tape record the profound teachings of this unique oral tradition as these teachings were given by Swamiji to his students in the form of lectures and oral translations. It is the essence of these teachings that is contained in the present volume, *Kashmir Śaivism: The Secret Supreme*.

By the time *Kashmir Śaivism: The Secret Supreme* was published in 1985, Swamiji had already translated and illuminated, and I had recorded, what he felt were the most important texts of Kashmir Śaivism. This tremendous work spanning almost fifteen years resulted in more than 450 hours of recordings. This included the translations and commentaries of the following texts:

Bhagavad Gītārthasamgraha
Bodhapañcadaśikā

Dehastadevatacakra Stotra
Janma Maraṇa Vicāra
Kuṇḍalinī Vijñāna Rahasyam
Paramarthasāraḥ
Parāprāveśikā
Parātrīṁśikā Laghuvṛitti
Parātrīṁśikā Vivaraṇa
Śiva Sūtra Vimarśinī
Śiva Stotrāvalī
Spanda Kārikā
Spanda Samdoha
Stavacintāmaṇi
Tantrāloka (18 chapters)
Vātūlanātha Sūtras
Vijñāna Bhairava

Under Swamiji's direct inspiration, the Universal Íaiva Fellowship, a fully accredited nonprofit organization, was established to realize his vision of making Kashmir Śaivism available to the whole world. This is being accomplished by preserving his teachings and making them available without the restriction of caste, creed or color in as many forms as possible. As more and more of the teachings of Kashmir Śaivism become available to the world, I feel proud and inspired that we are seeing the fulfillment of Swamiji's wishes.

John Hughes
Universal Shaiva Fellowship

Introduction to the First Edition

Due to events of the past, the tradition and teachings of Kashmir Śaivism have remained concealed for the past eight hundred years. Swami Lakshmanjoo is the last and the greatest of the Saints and Masters of this tradition. He is like a splendid and rare jewel. He has spent his whole life, beginning when he was a small boy, studying and practicing the teachings of this tradition and in so doing, has, due to his intellectual power and the strength of his awareness, realized both spiritually and intellectually the Reality of its thought.

In his teachings he constantly emphasizes the secular nature of this great tradition. He wants it to be clearly understood by everyone that Kashmir Śaivism does not discriminate against anyone on the basis of caste, creed, color, or sex. No one is restricted from becoming involved in the practice and teachings of this tradition. This teaching is universal, open to one and all.

The secret keys necessary for unlocking the treasury of knowledge which Kashmir Śaivism embodies have, since ancient times, been passed verbally from Master to disciple. It is this oral teaching which is the very life of this tradition and it is Swamiji who is the last living depository of this secret wealth. He is very concerned, therefore, that the reality of this tradition is not lost when he is gone from this world. It is with this in mind that, in the years 1971 and 1972, he gave the lectures which comprise this book. With Swamiji's direction and under his close supervision, these lectures were corrected by the Universal Shaiva Trust and are reproduced herein for the benefit and inspiration of all mankind.

John Hughes
Universal Shaiva Trust

Chapter One

Thirty-Six Elements
Tattvas

To begin with, I will explain to you the nature of that which is known as the *tattvas,* or elements. In *Vedānta* we are told that there are only twenty-five *tattvas*; however, in Śaivism we know that there are really thirty-six *tattvas*. These thirty six *tattvas* are the most important points for entering into Śaivism.

I will give the explanation of the *tattvas* in the manner of rising not descending . We must rise up to *Parama Śiva*. I prefer rising, not descending, so we must rise. I will, therefore, explain the grossest element 'earth' first and then proceed to explain subtler and subtler elements, until we reach the subtlest element, the finest, which is *Parama Śiva*.

36 *TATTVAS* – 36 ELEMENTS

Pañca mahābhūtas – Five Great Elements

pṛithvī	=	earth
jala	=	water
tejas	=	fire
vāyu	=	air
ākāśa	=	ether

Pañca tanmātras – Five Subtle Elements

gandha	=	smell
rasa	=	taste
rūpa	=	form
sparśa	=	touch
śabda	=	sound

Pañca karmendriyas – Five Organs of Action

upastha	=	creative
pāyu	=	excretion
pāda	=	foot
pāṇi	=	hand
vāk	=	speech

Pañca jñānendriyas – Five Organs of Cognition

ghrāṇa	=	nose, organ of smelling
rasanā	=	tongue, organ of tasting
cakṣu	=	eye, organ of seeing
tvak	=	skin, organ of touching
śrotra	=	ear, organ of hearing

Antaḥkaraṇas – Three Internal Organs

manas	=	mind
buddhiḥ	=	intellect
ahaṁkāra	=	ego connected with objectivity

prakṛiti	=	nature
puruṣa	=	ego connected with subjectivity

Ṣaṭ kañcukas – Six Coverings

niyati	=	limitation of place
kāla	=	limitation of time
rāga	=	limitation of attachment
vidyā	=	limitation of knowledge
kalā	=	limitation of action (creativity)
māyā	=	illusion of individuality

Śuddha tattvas – Pure Elements

śuddha vidyā	=	I-ness in I-ness—Thisness in Thisness
īśvara	=	Thisness in I-ness
sadāśiva	=	I-ness in Thisness
śakti	=	I-ness
śiva	=	I-ness (Being)

We will begin, therefore, from the lowest degree of the *tattvas*, which are the gross *tattvas*. The gross *tattvas* are called the *pañca–mahābhūtas*, the five great elements. They are the *tattvas* of *prithvī* (earth), *jala* (water), *tejas* (fire), *vāyu* (air), and *ākāśa* (ether). The element "ether" is not a perceptible element, such as the elements earth, air, fire, and water. Rather, it is space, unoccupied space. It gives you room to move. It is that element in which the other four gross elements have room to exist. We could say that it is a special vacuum which is filled by the other four great elements. These *tattvas* are gross and are called *mahābhūtas* (great elements) because the whole universe is based on these five elements.

After the five *mahābhūtas,* you move up to the five *tanmātras*. The five *tanmātras* correspond to the five *mahābhūtas*. *Gandha tanmātra* arises from the element of earth (*prithvī tattva*). The word *gandha* means "smell"; however, it is not exactly smell, it is the *abode* of smell, where smell lives. And that abode of smell is called *ganda tanmātra*. The next *tanmātra*, *rasa tanmātra*, has come out from the element of water (*jala mahābhūta*). *Rasa tanmātra* is the residence of the impression of taste (*rasa*). And then from the element of fire (*tejas mahābhūta*) issues forth *rūpa tanmātra*. Though the word *rūpa* means form, *rūpa tanmātra* is not exactly form; it is the residence of form, where the impression of form resides. This residence is called *rūpa tanmātra*. From the element of air (*vāyu mahābhūta*) rises *sparśa tanmātra,* which is the *tanmātra* of touch, the sensation of touch. This *tanmātra* is the residence of the sensation of touch. And finally, rising from the element of ether (*ākāśa mahābhūta*) is *śabda tanmātra*, the *tanmātra* of sound. This is the residence of the sensation of sound.

After the five *tanmātras* come the five *tattvas,* which are known as the five *karmendriyas*, the five organs of action. These organs of action are *vāk*, *pāṇi*, *pāda*, *pāyu*, and *upastha*. The first *karmendriya* is *vāk tattva*, the organ of speech. Next is *pāṇi tattva*. The word *pāṇi* means "hand." *Pāṇi* is that organ of action by which you take and give. Then comes *pāda tattva*. The word *pāda* means "foot." It is the organ by which you move about. It is the organ of locomotion. Next is *pāyu tattva,* which is the active organ of excretion. It is the organ of passing stools. The fifth and last *karmendriya* is *upastha tattva*. *Upastha tattva* is that *karmendriya*, that organ of action which is the active organ of sex and urination, the organ by which sex is performed and by which one urinates.

The next five *tattvas* are the five organs of cognition (knowledge) and are known as the five *jñānendriyas*. These are the mental organs with which we experience the world. These five organs are *ghrāṇa*, *rasanā*, *cakṣu*, *tvak*, and *śrotra*. The first *jñānendriya* is *ghrāṇa tattva*. The word *ghrāṇa* means "nose." The use of the word nose does not refer to breathing;

rather, nose is used here to indicate smell. This is the organ of cognition by which you smell. It creates odors. The next *tattva* is *rasanā tattva*. *Rasanā* means "tongue." Here the use of the word tongue does not refer to speech but to taste because, athough speech also comes from the tongue, it is an organ of action, not an organ of cognition. *Rasanā tattva* is that organ of cognition by which you taste. It creates flavors. Now follows *cakṣu tattva*. The word *cakṣu* means "eye." It is that organ of cognition by which you see. It creates form (*rūpaḥ*). The fourth *jñānendriya* is *tvak tattva*. *Tvak* means "skin." It is the organ of cognition by which you feel. It creates touch. The last organ of cognition is *śrotra tattva*. *Śrotra* means "ear." It is that organ of cognition by which you hear. It creates sound.

All of the above twenty elements;—the five *mahābhūtas*, the five *tanmātras*, the five *karmendriyas*, and the five *jñānendriyas*,—are called gross elements. They are all objective elements. The following elements, as we continue rising in our explanation of the *tattvas*, are said to be objective cum subjective elements. You should understand though that, in Śaivism, all the elements are really objective elements. They are called objects. Only that Super Being is subjective. Yet, as the following elements are a bit more connected to subjectivity than the former, we say that they are objective cum subjective elements.

Now we rise to the three *tattvas* which are known as the *antaḥkaraṇas*. The word *antaḥkaraṇas* means "internal organs." The three internal organs are *manas* (mind), *buddhiḥ* (intellect), and *ahaṁkāra* (ego).

Manas tattva, the element of mind, is said in Sanskṛit to be *saṁkalpasādhana*, the means by which you create thought. This could be any thought, such as, "I am going there, I will go there, I have done this, I have done that." This is the action of *manas*. The action of *buddhiḥ tattva*, the element of intellect, is to confirm whether I should do this or not. This is the field of the confirmation of the rightness of any proposed action, whether intellectual or moral, because, first, you must determine the rightness of a proposed decision or action and then make a choice dependent on this rightness. You ask yourself internally, "Should I perform this action or not? Is this the right decision or not?" The *buddhi* will reply to you, "No, you should not do it," or "Yes, you should do it." "This is bad, it is wrong to do it." "This is good, you should do it." "This answer is right, this answer is wrong." All this is done by the intellect.

Ahaṁkāra tattva is the element of ego which is connected with objectivity. When you attribute any action or knowledge to your self, such as, "I have done this and it was a mistake, I have done that and I ought not to have done it," or "I did a wonderful thing today which will benefit me a lot," this is the action of *ahaṁkāra tattva*. It creates limited "I" consciousness, the limited ego which is connected with objectivity.

Rising still further, we come to the two *tattvas* of *prakṛiti* and *puruṣa*. These two *tattvas* are interdependent. *Prakṛiti* is dependent upon *puruṣa* and *puruṣa* is dependent upon *prakṛiti*. *Prakṛiti* is the element which is known as "nature." It is the field where the three tendencies arise and flow forth. These three tendencies are known as the three *guṇas*, the three qualities. They are, respectively *sattva*, *rajas*, and *tamas*. *Prakṛiti* is the combination of these three *guṇas* but without any distinction. The three *guṇas* emerge from *prakṛiti* and thus it is said that the three *guṇas* are not in the field of the *tattvas*. They are not to be considered as *tattvas* because they are created by *prakṛiti*. *Tattvas* are creators, they are not created. It is, therefore, not the *guṇas* which are *tattvas* but their creator *prakṛiti*. And that which responds to that *prakṛiti*, which owns that *prakṛiti*, is called *puruṣa*.

Up to this point, I have explained twenty-five *tattvas*; five *mahābhūtas*, five *tanmātras*, five *karmendriyas*, five *jñānen-*

driyas, three *antaḥkaraṇas*, *prakṛiti*, and *puruṣa*. This is the limit of the *Vedāntin's* understanding of the *tattvas*. They say that there are only twenty-five *tattvas*. Yet in Śaivism, nothing as yet has happened. All these *tattvas* exist in the field of *māyā*, in the field of objectivity.

In Śaivism, *puruṣa* is not a realized soul. *Puruṣa tattva* is bound and limited just as *ahaṁkāra tattva* is. The only difference between *puruṣa* and *ahaṁkāra* is that *puruṣa* is connected with subjectivity and *ahaṁkāra* is connected with objectivity. And this *puruṣa* is entangled and bound in five ways, which are the five *kañcukas: niyati*, *kāla*, *rāga*, *vidyā*, and *kalā*.

First, there is *niyati tattva*. The function of *niyati tattva* is to put the impression in *puruṣa* that he is residing in a particular place and not in all places. You are residing in a houseboat near the First Bridge and you are not residing simultaneously at Ishiber near Nishat. You are residing in Kashmir; you are not residing simultaneously in Australia or Canada. This is the limitation which *niyati tattva* causes for *puruṣa*; that one is residing in a particular place and not everywhere.

Next comes *kāla tattva*. The word *kāla* means "time." The action of *kāla tattva* is to keep *puruṣa* in a particular period, the victim of being in a particular period. For instance, you are 25 years old, I am 64 years old, and he is 43 years old. This limitation is the result of the action of *kāla tattva*.

The third *tattva* by which *puruṣa* is limited is known as *rāga tattva*. *Rāga* means "attachment." This is that attachment which results from not being full. The action of *rāga tattva* is to leave the impression in *puruṣa* that he is not full, that he is not complete, and that he must have this or that to become full. He feels a lack which he must fill. This is the function of *rāga tattva* in limiting *puruṣa*.

The fourth *tattva* which limits *puruṣa* is *vidyā tattva*. *Vidyā* means "knowledge." The action of *vidyā tattva* is to put the impression in *puruṣa* that he has this or that particular and limited knowledge, that he is not all-knowing for he knows only some limited things.

The fifth and final bondage and limitation for *puruṣa* is *kalā tattva. Kalā tattva* creates the impression in *puruṣa* that he has some particular creativity, some particular artistic talent. He has mastered the art of writing, or the art of music, or the art of medicine; however, he does not have unlimited creativity. He is good at some things and not all things.

These five bondages of *puruṣa* are caused by *puruṣa's* ignorance of his own nature. And this ignorance is another *tattva*, which is known as *māyā tattva*. These five *tattvas* are created by *māyā* for *puruṣa*. That *puruṣa* who is the victim of *māyā*, therefore, does not know his own real nature and becomes bound and entangled by these five (*kañcukas*) and thus becomes a victim of *prakṛiti*. He takes on individuality and becomes a limited individual.

These five *tattvas* plus *māyā* are known as *ṣat kañcukas* (the six-fold coverings). These are the six coverings which bind and entangle and, therefore, limit *puruṣa*. He is not limited by only one covering but by six and these coverings must be removed, and this is done automatically by the grace of the Master. Through this grace, at the time of real knowledge, *māyā* is transformed into His *śakti*, His great energy. In His glory, *māyā* becomes the glory of *Parama Śiva*. When *puruṣa* realizes the reality of his nature, *māyā* becomes glory for him.

We have completed our examination of those *tattvas*, from the *antaḥkaraṇas* to *māyā*, which are connected with objectivity cum subjectivity. We will now rise to those *tattvas* which are connected with pure subjectivity. This is the subjective course to be entered into by *puruṣa* for rising from pure subjectivity to purer subjectivity to purest subjectivity.

Pure subjectivity is found in the *tattva* known as *śuddhavidyā tattva*. This exists when *puruṣa* actually realizes his own nature. And yet that realization is not stable; it is flickering, it is moving. This is the realization at the level of *śuddhavidyā tattva*. This realization is in motion. Sometimes you realize it, sometimes you forget it. And the experience (*parāmarśa*) of *śuddhavidyā tattva* is, "I am *Śiva*, this universe is in duality. This universe is unreal, I am *Śiva*." This is the impression which comes in *śuddhavidyā tattva* and it is pure subjectivity.

Now purer subjectivity will come in the next two *tattvas*, *īśvara tattva* and *sadāśiva tattva*. In *īśvara tattva*, you realize, "This universe is my own expansion. This universe is not an illusion, it is my own expansion." The realization which takes place in *sadāśiva tattva* is the same as the realization which takes place in *īśvara tattva*, but more refined. In *sadāśiva tattva*, you realize,"I am this whole universe." This is the difference between these two impressions. In *īśvara tattva*, you have the impression, "This universe is my own expansion," whereas in *sadāśiva tattva*, you will find "I myself am this whole universe." These two *tattvas* comprise subjectivity in a purer form.

Now in the final two *tattvas*, we come to subjectivity in its purest form. These two *tattvas* are the interdependent *tattvas*: *śakti tattva* and *śiva tattva*. The impression which comes in these two *tattvas* is only I, the pure I, the universal I. It is not "this universe is my own expansion" or "I am this whole universe." No, it is just I, pure I, universal I.

Last is that Being which does not come in the cycle of *tattvas* that Being called *Parama Śiva*. *Parama Śiva* is not only found in *śiva tattva* or in *śakti tattva*. It is not only here, not only there. You will find It everywhere. You will find It from the lowest *tattva* to the highest. It is all levels, and therefore no level. It is everywhere, that is why It is nowhere. The one Being who is everywhere, It is nowhere.

Chapter Two

The Sixfold Path of the Universe
Ṣaḍadhvan

In Śaivism this objective universe is said to be threefold, because it is composed of three paths (*adhvans*). These *adhvans* are gross (*sthūla*), subtle (*sūkṣma*), and subtlest (*para*). The gross path is called *bhuvanādhva*, the subtle path *tattvādhva*, and the subtlest path *kalādhva*—first *bhuvanādhva*, then *tattvādhva*, and finally *kalādhva*.

The word *adhvan* means "path." Here, path has a twofold meaning: it is either that path on which you tread, or that path which you must dispose of, must discard. You have either to tread on the path or discard the path. You can dispose of this path only by the grace of your Master. And when you dispose of this path, you reach the state of *Parama Śiva*.

There is no question of realizing God through treading on this path. You may tread for centuries and centuries and still you will be treading. So you must discard this path, dispose of it. When you do dispose of the path, that is also called *adhvan*. Disposing of it, however, can only be done by the grace of the Master, who is the embodiment of *Parama Śiva*.

That path which is said to be gross is known as *bhuvanādhva*. *Bhuvanādhva* means "the path of all the worlds." In Śaivism, these worlds are said to number one hundred and eighteen. By one world, I do not mean one planet. This whole cosmos, including suns, moons, stars, and planets, is called one world. It has been found by *yogins* in *samādhi* that there are one hundred and eighteen worlds like this cosmos which have been created. This combination of one hundred and eighteen worlds is called *bhuvanādhva*.

The complete system of the thirty-six *tattvas*, which I have explained earlier, is called *tattvādhva*. *Tattvādhva* means "the course of all elements," the path of the *tattvas*. This is that path which is subtle.

That path (*adhvan*) which is more refined than *tattvādhva* is known as *kalādhva*. That path is the subtlest. *Kalādhva* consists of five *kalās,* which are five boundaries or enclosures. These *kalās* are enclosures for all of the thirty-six elements, the thirty-six *tattvas*, from earth up to *Śiva*. The first and outermost enclosure is called *nivṛitti kalā*. In *nivṛitti kalā* you will find the first *tattva*, *pṛithvī tattva*, the element "earth."

The next *kalā* or enclosure is *pratiṣṭhā kalā*. In *pratiṣṭhā kalā* you find the twenty-three *tattvas* from *jala tattva*, the element "water," up to and including *prakṛiti tattva*. The next enclosure is known as *vidyā kalā*. *Vidyā kalā* contains the seven *tattvas,* from *puruṣa tattva* up to and including *māyā tattva*. The next enclosure is called *śāntā kalā*. *Śāntā kalā* contains the four *tattvas* from *śuddhavidyā tattva* up to and including *śakti tattva*, the thirty-fifth *tattva*. The fifth and last enclosure is known as *śāntātītā kalā*. Here, you will only find the existence of *śiva tattva*.

This course of the threefold *adhvans* is called *vācyādhva*. The word *vācya* means "that which is observed, spoken, told." So *vācyādhva* is the path of that which is observed, seen, realized. It is called *vācyādhva* because it is seen, it is observed, it is created, it is felt. It is the objective cycle of this creation.

Now, we must turn to its observer, the creator of this *adhvan*. The creator of the threefold path of the universe known as *vācyādhva* is called *vācakādhva*. The meaning of the word *vācaka* is "that which observes, sees, and creates." And so that path which observes, sees, and creates is called *vācakādhva*. It is the subjective cycle of this creation. And, like *vācyādhva*, *vācakādhva*, is also composed of three paths: gross (*sthūla*), subtle (*sūkṣma*), and subtlest (*para*).

Gross (*sthūla*) *vācakādhva* is called *padādhva* and consists of sentences; sentences are said to be gross. Subtle (*sukṣma*) *vācakādhva* is called *mantrādhva* and consists of words, because words are known to be more subtle than sentences. Subtler than *mantrādhva*, the world of words, is the path of letters, called *varṇādhva*.

Take any object, such as a pot. That object will fall in the threefold world of *vācyādhva*. It is an offshoot of the thirty-six elements. On the other hand, the word "pot" is *vācakādhva* for this object. So, this object is *vācya* and its *vācaka* is the word "pot."

The combination of all of these six *adhvans*, the three objective *adhvans* and the three subjective *adhvans* is called *ṣaḍadhva*, the six fold *adhvans*. This is the explanation of this whole universe, both subjective and objective.

Chapter Three

The Theory of the Alphabet
Mātṛikācakra

Mātṛikācakra is the theory of the alphabet. This theory teaches us that the whole universe is created by God, Lord Śiva, as one with, and not separated from, His own nature. He has created this universe in His own Self as the reflection of His sweet will. The creation of this universe is the outcome of this reflection. In Śaivism the sweet will of God is known as *icchā śakti*, the energy of will. It is through His will that the reflection of the universe takes place in His own nature. This reflection, however, is not like that reflection which takes place in an ordinary mirror, where the mirror is the reflector and that which is reflected in the mirror is external to it. The reflection of the universe, which takes place in Lord Śiva's own nature, is like the reflection which takes place in a cup-shaped mirror. Here, Lord Śiva takes the form of a cup and puts another cup in front of His nature. And in that second cup, which is inseparable from Him, the reflection of the universe takes place.

This universe, as I explained earlier, is contained in the thirty-six elements, the thirty-six *tattvas*. And from the point of view of descending, first comes *śiva tattva*, then *śakti tattva*, then *sadāśiva tattva*, then *īśvara tattva*, then *śuddhavidyā tattva*, then *māyā tattva*, and so forth. Yet the reflection of the universe does not take place in this descending manner, from *śiva tattva* to *māyā tattva*, etc. Rather, it takes place in a reverse fashion. The reflection of the universe takes place from *pṛithvī tattva*, the element earth, to *śakti tattva*, from the lowest to the highest, not from the highest to the lowest. Just as in the ordinary course of experience when you see your face in a concave mirror, your head will appear as down and your body will appear as up. In the same way, this whole universe begins from *śakti tattva*, but it is experienced as beginning from *pṛithvī tattva*. The lowest element earth is reflected first and then the element water, then fire (*agni*), then air (*vāyu*), and so on, up to *śakti tattva*.

And so, even though the real way in which the universe is expanded is from *śiva tattva* to *śakti tattva* and so on, this reflection makes you feel as if the lowest element, earth, is reflected first. And this is due to the fact that it *is* reflected. It is the reflection that makes you feel this way because this reflection is an inseparable reflection. There is no mirror outside separate from that which is reflected in the mirror. In the ordinary course of life, you experience that which is reflected in the mirror is at one place and the mirror, which is the reflector, is at another. In the reflection of the universe, however, the reflected and the reflector are inseparable. It is Śiva and His Śakti, the energy holder and His energy, His energy of will.

Lord Śiva, the reflector of this whole universe, is full of five energies, and these five energies are *cit śakti*, the energy of consciousness; *ānanda śakti*, the energy of bliss; *icchā śakti*, the energy of will; *jñāna śakti*, the energy of knowledge; and *kriyā śakti*, the energy of action.

These five energies are represented in the sixteen vowels of the Sanskṛit alphabet: *a, ā, i, ī, u, ū, ṛi, ṛī, li, lī, e, ai, o, au, ṁ, ḥ*, which comprise *śiva tattva*.

The first letter of the Sanskṛit alphabet, *a*, represents *cit śakti*, the energy of consciousness of Lord Śiva. The second letter of the Sanskṛit alphabet, the letter *ā*, represents *ānanda śakti*, the energy of bliss of Lord Śiva. *Cit śakti* and *ānanda śakti*, the energies of consciousness and bliss, are totally inseparable. Where there is consciousness (*cit*), there is bliss (*ānanda*), and where there is bliss, there is consciousness. Here, at this stage, the universe has not yet taken shape. It is only residing in *ānanda śakti*, the energy of bliss.

After *cit śakti* and *ānanda śakti* comes *icchā śakti*, the energy of will. *Icchā śakti* is represented by the third and fourth letters of the alphabet, the letters *i* and *ī*. You must understand that *icchā śakti* is not desire—it is will. It is wrong understanding to think of *icchā śakti* as the energy of desire. It is the power of will. And this *icchā śakti* takes two forms: unagitated and agitated. In its unagitated form, *icchā śakti* resides peacefully in its own nature and is represented by the letter *i*. Next, the agitated formation of *icchā śakti* takes place. This state is represented by the next letter of the alphabet, the letter *ī*. This is the state of agitated will. In this state, Lord Śiva's will is agitated but not in such a way that it is separated from His own nature. It remains as residing in His own consciousness and bliss, *cit* and *ānanda*.

At this point the apprehension takes place in Lord Śiva's consciousness that if I go forward, if I move onwards, I may lose my own nature. And this apprehension takes place in *jñāna śakti*, the energy of knowledge of Lord Śiva, and is represented in the next two letters of the alphabet, the letters *u* and *ū*. The first of these two letters, the letter *u*, is called *unmeṣa*. The word *unmeṣa* indicates that the universal existence is about to begin, it is just forthcoming. It has not yet begun, it is not yet created, it is about to be created. And when He begins to create the universe, He becomes apprehensive and this apprehension is known as *ūnatā,* which means "lessening." This state is represented by the letter *ū*. It is that state in which Lord Śiva has the foreboding that His *cit śakti* and *ānanda śakti* may be decreased if He continues to move out to create the universe. This feeling keeps Him at a standstill and prevents His moving forward.

He, therefore, discards the universe. He separates the universe from His own nature and resides in His own *cit śakti* and *ānanda śakti*, consciousness and bliss. This state, wherein Lord Śiva has rejected the universe and is only residing in His own nature of consciousness and bliss, is represented by the next four vowels of the alphabet, the letters *ṛi, ṛī, li,* and *lī*. The state that these four vowels indicate is that state where the Supreme, filled with consciousness and bliss, resides in His own nature. He does not move out. Because of this, there is no possibility of the universe coming into manifestation. Here the manifestation of the universe totally stops. Hence, these four vowels, *ṛi, ṛī, li,* and *lī,* are called *amṛita bīja*, which means "residing in His own bliss (*ānanda*)." At this stage, there is no thought of creating the universe. These four vowels do not create anything. The state of Lord Śiva which these four vowels represent is known as *anāśrita śiva. Anāśrita śiva* refers to that Śiva who has not accepted the existence of the universe in His own nature. In this state, Lord Śiva resides in His own nature forever.

The apprehension "If I create this universe I may lose My own nature" is known as *ūnatā*. It came out from the agitated state of the *jñāna śakti* of Lord Śiva. Yet the first two energies of Lord Śiva, *cit śakti* and *ānanda śakti*, the energies of consciousness and bliss, do not recognize this apprehension. These two energies are at ease. They understand that to create this universe is only the glory of His nature; therefore, why be apprehensive? There is no question of apprehension arising in

Lord Śiva. Why, therefore, should He be frightened about coming out? Coming out or going in is the same to Him. As these two energies, *cit śakti* and *ānanda śakti*, have this understanding, therefore, they begin anew to create this universe.

So *cit śakti* and *ānanda śakti*, the energies of consciousness and bliss, which are represented in the vowels *a* and *ā*, create contact with *icchā śakti*, the energy of will, which is represented in the vowels *i* and *ī* and create the letter *e*. And then simultaneously *cit śakti* and *ānanda śakti* contact *e* and give rise to the letter *ai*. And when *cit śakti* and *ānanda śakti* come in contact with *jñāna śakti*, the energy of knowledge, represented in the letters *u* and *ū*, they create the letter *o*. And when simultaneously *cit śakti* and *ānanda śakti* contact the letter *o*, they give rise to the letter *au*. So when *a* or *ā* come in contact with *i* or *ī*, the letter *e* is created. And when *a* or *ā* come in contact with the letter *e*, the letter *ai* is created. In the same way, when *a* or *ā* comes in contact with *u* or *ū*, the letter *o* is created. And when *a* and *ā* come in contact with *o*, the letter *au* is created.

These four letters, *e, ai, o, au*, which were created by the contact of *cit śakti* and *ānanda śakti* with *icchā śakti* and *jñāna śakti*, represent the four states of *kriyā śakti*, the energy of action of Lord Śiva. The first state of the energy of action, which is represented by the letter *e*, is called *asphuṭa* (not vivid) *kriyā śakti*. In this state, the energy of action is not clear. In the next state of *kriyā śakti*, which is represented by the letter *ai*, the energy of action becomes *sphuṭa* (vivid). In the third state of *kriyā śakti*, represented by the letter *o*, the energy of action becomes *sphuṭatara* (more vivid). And in the fourth and final movement and state of *kriyā śakti*, represented by the letter *au*, the energy of action becomes *sphuṭatama* (most vivid). So the energy of action has four states as represented in the letters *e, ai, o,* and *au*. And in these four states, the energy of action begins as not vivid (*asphuṭa kriyā śakti*), then becomes vivid (*sphuṭa kriyā śakti*), then more vivid (*sphuṭatara kriyā śakti*), and finally most vivid (*sphuṭatama kriyā śakti*). In this energy of action, the reflection of the whole universe takes place. Although this universe is reflected in His total energy of action, yet this reflection has taken place primarily in His fourth energy of action, which is represented by the letter *au*.

The fact is, however, that even though this whole universe has been created, the nature of His Self, which is full of consciousness and bliss, has not been lessened at all. Nothing has happened. He is only residing in His own point. This state of Lord Śiva is represented by the letter *ṁ* (*anusvāra*). The letter *ṁ*, therefore, shows that the existence of Lord Śiva has not moved from His own nature, even though this whole universe is created in His Self.

The reflection of the universe, which has been explained earlier as being in the form of a cup-shaped mirror, is represented by the sixteenth letter of the Sanskṛit alphabet, *visarga*, the letter *ḥ*. In *devanāgarī* script the letter *ḥ* takes the form of the two points of the colon ":." And these two points of the *visarga* (:) represent the two cups in which the reflection of the universe takes place. These two points are known as *śiva bindu* and *śakti bindu*.

I have explained that the Sanskṛit vowels, from the letter *a*, which is *anuttara*, to the letter *ḥ*, which is *visarga*, are *śiva tattva*. The remainder of the alphabet is *śakti tattva*, the universe of thirty-five *tattvas*. And this universe is the reflection of His *svātantrya*. It is not created, it is a reflection. You may ask, if they are not created, then how is each succeeding letter produced? Are they produced just by reflecting against the letter or are they produced from within their own self? The answer is, they are not produced in either of these ways. Actually, it is the reflection of *svātantrya* that gives rise to each succeeding letter. In *cit śakti*, *ānanda śakti*, *icchā śakti*, *jñāna śakti*, and *kriyā śakti,* the *svātantrya* of Lord Śiva is reflected. All of the elements (*tattvas*) are a reflection of the five energies of Lord Śiva. No element escapes these five energies. Everything comes out from these five energies. It is His *svātantrya* that, from these five energies, first come the five *mahābhūtas*, and then come the five *tanmātras*, and then come the five *karmendriyas*, and so on. And in each of these energies all of the five energies exist. For example, in *cit śakti,* all the five energies, *cit śakti*, *ānanda śakti*, *icchā śakti*, *jñāna śakti*, and *kriyā śakti*, are present. At the same time, you should understand that although in one energy all the energies are present, only one energy is predominant. So five energies into five energies is twenty-five and these are the first twenty-five *tattvas*, from *pṛithvī* to *puruṣa*.

The five *mahābhūtas*, which are the five consonants from *ṅa* to *ka*, are produced by *cit śakti* (*anuttara*) and *ānanda śakti*, which are one and are the letters *a* and *ā*, when mixed with His five energies. That reflection where His *cit śakti* is predominant is *ākāśa* (ether) and this is the letter *ṅa*.[1] The reflection of His *ānanda śakti* is *vāyu* (air) and this is the letter *gha*. The reflection of His *icchā śakti* is *agni* (fire) and this is the letter *ga*. The reflection of His *jñāna śakti* is *jala* (water) and this is the letter *kha*. And the reflection of His *kriyā śakti* is *pṛithvī* (earth) and this is the letter *ka*.

The five *tanmātras*, which are the consonants from *ña* to *ca*, are produced by *icchā śakti*, the letters *i* and *ī*, when it is mixed with the five energies. That reflection where His *cit śakti* is predominant is *śabda*, the residence of sound, and this is the letter *ña*. The reflection of His *ānanda śakti* is *sparśa*, the residence of touch, and this is the letter *jha*. The reflection of His

1 *Śakti tattva* is a reflection of *Śiva tattva*. The reflective flow, therefore, is in each case from the last letter to the first letter, e.g., from *ṅa* to *ka*, and the order of the consonants is reversed.

icchā śakti is *rūpa*, the residence of form, and this is the letter *ja*. The reflection of His *jñāna śakti* is *rasa*, the residence of taste, and this is the letter *cha*. And the reflection of His *kriyā śakti* is *gandha*, the residence of smell, and this is the letter *ca*.

The five *karmendriyas*, which are the five consonants from *ṇa* to *ṭa*, are produced by the letters *ṛi* and *ṛī*, which is *anaśṛitaśiva*, in conjunction with the five energies. The five *jñānendriyas*, which are the five consonants from *na* to *ta*, are produced by the same tattva through the letters *li* and *lī*.

The five *karmendriyas* are reflected as follows. The reflection where His *cit śakti* is predominant is *vāk*, the organ of speech, and this is the letter *ṇa*. The reflection of His *ānanda śakti* is *pāṇi*, the organ of action, and this is the letter *ḍha*. The reflection of His *icchā śakti* is *pāda*, the organ of locomotion, and this is the letter *ḍa*. The reflection of His *jñāna śakti* is *pāyu*, the organ of excretion, and this is the letter *ṭha*. And the reflection of His *kriyā śakti* is *upastha*, the active organ of sex, and this is the letter *ṭa*.

The five *jñānendriyas* are reflected in the following manner. The reflection where His cit *śakti* is predominant is *śrotra*, the cognitive organ of hearing, and this is the letter *na*. The reflection of His *ānanda śakti* is *tvak*, the cognitive organ of touch, and this is the letter *dha*. The reflection of His *icchā śakti* is *cakṣu*, the cognitive organ of sight, and this is the letter *da*. The reflection of His *jñāna śakti* is *rasanā*, the cognitive organ of taste, and this is the letter *tha*. And the reflection of His *kriyā śakti* is *ghrāṇa*, the cognitive organ of smell, and this is the letter *ta*.

Jñāna śakti, which is the letters *u* and *ū*, when mixed with the five energies, produces the five elements *manas, ahaṁkāra, buddhi, prakṛiti,* and *puruṣa*, which are the five consonants from *pa* to *ma*. That reflection where His *cit śakti* is predominant is *puruṣa*, the limited self, and this is the letter *ma*. The reflection of His *ānanda śakti* is *prakṛiti*, nature, and this is the letter *bha*. The reflection of His *icchā śakti* is *buddhi*, intellect, and this is the letter *ba*. The reflection of His *jñāna śakti* is *ahaṁkāra*, ego, and this is the letter *pha*. And the reflection of His *kriyā śakti* is *manas*, mind, and this is the letter *pa*.

The six internal states of *puruṣa*, which are *māyā, kalā, vidyā, rāga, kāla,* and *niyati*, are reduced to four by combining *niyati* with *rāga* and *kāla* with *kalā*. The four limitations which result from these combinations correspond to the next four semi-vowels *ya, ra, la* and *va*. The limitations *kāla* and *kalā*, which are the limitations of time and creativity, correspond to the letter *ya*. *Vidyā*, limited knowledge, corresponds to the letter *ra*; *rāga* and *niyati*, the limitations of attachment and space, to *la*; and *māyā*, the element of self ignorance and objectivity, corresponds to *va*.

It cannot be said that these limitations are created by the energies of Lord Śiva as they represent the internal state of *puruṣa*. These limitations, therefore, are called *antaḥstha* because they reside inside *puruṣa*, one's own limited self. They are the internal state of limited *puruṣa*.

The four *tattvas—śuddhavidyā, īśvara, sadāśiva*, and *śakti*—are also not created by the energies of Lord Śiva. Instead, they are the swelling of the heat of His own nature. *Śuddhavidyā*, which is the state of *ahaṁ-ahaṁ /idaṁ-idaṁ* (I-I / this-this), is the letter *śa*. *Īśvara*, which is the state of *idaṁ-ahaṁ* (this-I), is the letter *ṣa*. *Sadāśiva*, which is the state of *ahaṁ-idaṁ* (I-this), is the letter *sa*. *Śakti*, which is the state of *ahaṁ* (I), is the letter *ha*. This is the reason that these four letters in grammar are called *ūṣma*, which means "the heat of His own nature." They are the expansion of the state of unlimited Being and, as such, are attached to the unlimited state of *puruṣa*, which is the expansion of that state of unlimited Being.

The great Sanskṛit grammarian Pāṇini also explains the alphabet as we do in our Śaivism.

akuhavisarjanīyānāṁ kaṇṭhaḥ /

The place where the following letters are produced is the throat:

a, ā, ka, kha, ga, gha, ṅa, ha, ḥ

icuyaśānāṁ tālu /

The place where the following letters are produced is the soft palate:

i, ī, ca, cha, ja, jha, ña, ya, śa

riṭurasāṇāṁ mūrdhā /

The place where the following letters are produced is the head:

ṛi, ṛī, ṭa, ṭha, ḍa, ḍha, ṇa, ra, ṣa

litulasānāṁ dantāḥ /

The place where the following letters are produced is the teeth:

li, lī, ta, tha, da, dha, na, la, sa

upūpadhmānīyānāmoṣṭhau /

The place where the following letters are produced is the lips:

u, ū, pa, pha, ba, bha, ma, upadhmānīya[2]

ñamaṅaṇanānāṁ nāsikā ca /

The place where the following letters are produced is the nose:

ña, ṅa, ṇa, na, ma

edaitoḥ kaṇṭhatālu /

The following letters are produced by the throat and palate:

e, ai

2. *upadhmānīya* is used in the recitation of *mantras* in the *Vedas*.

odautoḥ kaṇṭhoṣṭam /

The following letters are produced by the throat and lips:

o, au

vakārasya dantoṣṭham /

The following letter is produced by the teeth and lips:

va

jihvāmūlīyasya jihvāmūlam /

From the root of the tongue is produced:

jihvāmūlīya[3]

nāsikānusvārasya /

From the nose is produced:

ṁ - anusvāra

The aim of *mātṛikācakra* is to function with the first and the last letter in either the way of Śiva or the way of Śakti. To function in the way of Śiva, take the first letter *a* which is the first step of Lord Śiva in the creative field, and combine this with the last state of Lord Śiva, the letter *ha*, which is the resting place and the last letter of *mātṛikācakra*. This also corresponds to Pāṇini's concept of *pratyāhāra*. Take the first letter along with the last letter and you will find that all of the letters are existing therein. The whole universe of letters falls within these two letters.

According to the rules of Sanskṛit grammar, we then, after combining the letters *a* and *ha*, have to append the letter *ṁ* on the end and this creates the *mantra* of Lord Śiva, the *mantra aham̐*.[4] The letter *ṁ* has a special significance. It indicates that this whole *pratyāhāra*, which is contained in the letters from *a* to *ha*, and which has produced the one hundred and eighteen worlds, the thirty-six elements, and the five circles (*kalās*), has

---

3 The guttural class of consonants uttered from the root of the tongue.

4 *Ahaṁ* is the *mantra* of Universal "I."

in reality created nothing. It is just one point. This is the significance of the letter *ṁ*, which is *anusvāra*.

The way of Śakti is the way of energy. The difference between Śakti *pratyāhāra* and Śiva *pratyāhāra* is that in Śakti *pratyāhāra,* two Śaktis combine and create a world of their own. Śakti is actually the existence of created Being. Śiva is the creator. Here, Śakti wants to become independent of Śiva. To do so, She must create a world of Her own. It is like what happens with bees. When the queen bee stops creating eggs, then the worker bees, without mating, create eggs of their own. This is the mating of Śaktis. Śiva is put aside and Śakti combines with Śakti to create their own world, which is the expansion of Śaktis. And this creation takes the first letter of the consonants, the letter *ka*, which is the first letter of the Śaktis and combines it with the last letter of the Śaktis, the last consonant, the letter *sa*[5] and produces the *mantra* of Śakti, the *mantra kṣa*.

In the kingdom of *mātṛikācakra,* there exists three kinds of *visargas*, three kinds of flow. These three *visargas* are known as *śāmbhava visarga*, *śākta visarga*, and *āṇava visarga*.

The first *visarga* exists at the stage of *ānanda śakti,* and is represented by the letter *ā*. This *visarga* is known as *śāmbhava visarga*. The mode of this *visarga* is said to be *cittapralayaḥ*. The word *cittapralayaḥ* indicates that state where your mind does not function, where only thoughtlessness exists. Here the mind does not work at all. This is the thoughtless flow. This *śāmbhava visarga* is also known as *parā visarga*, the supreme *visarga*. This supreme *visarga* is concerned with Śiva.

The second *visarga* is known as *śākta visarga*. It is also

5 The letter "*ha*" is not part of this creation of the *Śaktis* because *ha* is a letter which is attached to Śiva and, therefore, *śakti* does not recognize her nature without Śiva. The letter *ha* is *apara visarga*, the gross *visarga* of Lord Śiva.

known as *parāparā visarga*, the highest cum lowest or medium *visarga*. This *visarga* is represented by the last letter of the vowels, the letter *ḥ* which in grammar is also designated as *visargaḥ*. The mode of this *visarga* is called *cittasaṁbodhaḥ*. *Cittasaṁbodhaḥ* indicates that state where awareness is maintained in one-pointedness.

The third and last *visarga* is called *āṇava visarga*. It is also known as *aparā visargaḥ*, the lower or inferior *visarga*. It is the *visarga* of the individual (*naraḥ*). This *visarga* is attributed to the letter *ha*, the last letter of the Sanskṛit alphabet. The mode of this *visarga* is called *cittaviśrāntiḥ*. The word *cittaviśrāntiḥ* indicates that state where the mind rests in concentration, where the mind takes a permanent seat in concentration.

Chapter Four

The Theory of Reflection
Pratibimbavādaḥ

In the ordinary worldly course, sound is reflected outwardly in ether and inwardly in the ear. Touch is reflected outwardly in air and inwardly in the skin. Form is reflected outwardly in fire and in a mirror and inwardly in the eye. Taste is reflected outwardly in water and inwardly in the tongue. Smell is reflected outwardly in the earth and inwardly in the nose. These reflections, however, are just like the reflections in a mirror. They only take place individually. All five reflections are not available at once; only one thing is reflected in each. In a mirror, form is reflected. Touch can not be reflected in a mirror nor can taste, smell, or sound. A mirror will only reflect form. It is only in Supreme God Consciousness that you find all five reflected at once. In fact, although these reflections are experienced individually in all of the sense organs—sight in the eye, sound in the ear, etc.—these reflections could not even be observed if consciousness were not there. Awareness is needed and this is found in consciousness, not in the organs.

The universe, therefore, is reflected in the mirror of consciousness, not in the organs nor in the five gross elements. These are merely *tattvas* and cannot reflect anything. The real reflector is consciousness. In consciousness, however, you see only the reflected thing and not the object that is reflected. That which is reflected (*bimba*) is, in fact, *svātantrya*. This whole universe is the reflection of *svātantrya*[1] in God Consciousness. There is no additional class of similar objects existing outside of this world that He reflects in His nature. The outside element, that which is reflected, is only *svātantrya*. The infinite variety which is created is only the expansion of *svātantrya*.[2]

You can understand this by taking the example of cause and effect. When a potter makes a pot, he takes clay and gives form to that clay with his potter's instruments, such as a stick, a string, and the potter's wheel. Within the potter's creative activity, two kinds of causes can be distinguished. There is the material cause, which in Sanskṛit is called *upādānakāraṇa*. This is that cause that travels with the effect. It cannot and does not become separated from the effect. Second, there is the formal cause, which in Sanskṛit is called *nimittakāraṇa*. The formal cause does not travel with the effect. The material cause is the potter's clay and the formal cause is the potter himself and his stick, string, and wheel. In the ordinary worldly course, the object which is reflected (*bimba*) seems to be the cause of the reflection (*pratibimba*) because the reflection cannot exist without that which is reflected. We have seen, however, that all reflection is really a reflection in God Consciousness. If the object reflected is really the cause of the reflection, then what kind of cause is it? Is it the material cause, which travels with

1 *Svātantrya śakti* is one with God Consciousness. There are not two elements, such as the mirror and the object which is reflected in the mirror. The reflected and the reflection are one. The mirror, which is the absolutely independent will of God (*svātantrya*), is God Consciousness.

2 yadvāpi kāraṇaṁ kiñcit bimbatvena...
Tantrāloka: III;50

the effect, or is it the formal cause, which does not travel with the effect? It cannot be the material cause because that would mean that there is something outside of God Consciousness which travels to become part of the effect which is the reflection. It is our theory in Śaivism that nothing can exist outside of God Consciousness. There cannot, therefore, be any agency which is separate from God Consciousness and which travels with the cause because if it is separate from God Consciousness and therefore from the effect, it would not exist.

If the reflection of some object is existing in the mirror of God Consciousness, then what is that reflection a reflection of? We have seen that if the object which is reflected were to remain outside of God Consciousness, then it would not exist. There can be nothing, therefore, which is outside to be reflected in the mirror of God Consciousness. There is only the mirror. There is no external cause which has gone into the reflection which is the effect. There is only the mirror of God Consciousness.

But what then is the cause of this reflection? *Svātantrya* is the mirror. *Svātantrya*, the absolutely independent will of God, is the cause of this reflection. Unlike ordinary reflection which we experience in the world wherein an object can be distinguished as the cause of that reflection, in God Consciousness only the reflection exists and not anything that is separate and reflected (*bimba*). In this causality, *svātantrya* is the formal cause (*nimittakāraṇa*), not the material cause (*upādānakāraṇa*), of the reflection. It does not travel from the cause into the effect because, as I have explained, there is no cause which could be separate from God Consciousness. It is His free will that He wills and what He wills appears in the mirror of His Consciousness. It is simply His will (*svātantrya*). In reality, only the reflection exists and not anything that is reflected.

This universe, therefore, is found in the reflector of God Consciousness, not through the agency of anything of which it is a reflection (*bimba*) but through His *svātantrya,* where the universe is contained in seed form. *Svātantrya* is the seed of everything. Everything exists in the mirror of God Consciousness with *svātantrya* as its cause.

The theory of reflection (*pratibimbavāda*) is meant for advanced *yogins*. This theory teaches them how to be aware in their daily activities, while talking, while walking, while tasting, while touching, while hearing, while smelling. While they are performing all of these various actions, they see that all of these actions move in their Supreme Consciousness. Their vision, their perception, heretofore limited, becomes unlimited. The mode of their actions becomes absolutely unique. They see each and every action in their God Consciousness. They exist in the state of *sadāśiva*. Each and every action of their life becomes glorious. This is the awareness that comes from the practice of *pratibimba*.

Chapter Five

The Explanation of the Means
Upāyas

The meaning of the Sanskṛit word *upāya* is "means." The word *upāya* in Kashmir Śaivism is used to indicate the means to enter into Universal God Consciousness from individual consciousness. Our Śaivism proclaims that there are three means for entering into Universal God Consciousness: *śāmbhavopāya*, the supreme means; *śāktopāya*, the medium means; and *āṇavopāya*, the inferior means.

Śāmbhavopāya

Śāmbhavopāya, the supreme means, functions in *mātṛikācakra*, *pratyāhāra*, and *pratibimbavāda*. The definition given in the "*Mālinīvijayottaratantram*" for *śāmbhavopāya* is "the one who preserves thoughtlessness." By preserving thoughtlessness, that is, not having thoughts and maintaining the continuity of that thoughtlessness, and by the grace of the Master, one enters into that transcendental consciousness where he finds that this whole universe has come out from sentences and sentences from words and words from letters and letters from that real "I" which is *Parama Śiva*. Here, one finds that this whole universe is reflected in his own consciousness and that it is reflected from within rather than from without.[1]

Śāmbhavopāya is called *icchopāya* because it originates from *icchā śakti* and because it is that means which exists in the state of the meant. In *śāmbhavopāya,* there are no means to travel upon. It is the meant. There is nowhere to go. You must reside only in the meant. The rest is automatic. Here, only the grace of your Master is necessary. It must be realized, however, that you yourself must come to this point where you reside in the meant and this you do by maintaining the continuity of thoughtlessness. Up to this point, therefore, there is still something to be done. When you reside only in the meant, it is then the grace of your Master that carries you. You must reach that state where only your Master shines for you. This means that you must merge in your Master's consciousness. In this state, you do not exist; only your Master exists. Masters select disciples for this *upāya* who are highly developed in awareness. Until then, they will not be accepted by the Master for this *upāya*. In this *upāya,* the Master functions more than does the disciple.

In our Kashmir Śaivism, we say,

svamuktimātre kasyāpi
yāvadviśvavimocane |
pratibhodeti khadyota-
ratnatārendu sūryavat ||

Tantraloka: XIII:159

---

1 akiṁciccintakasyaiva guruṇā pratibodhataḥ |
jāyate yaḥ samāveśaḥ śāmbhavo 'sāvudīritaḥ ||

Mālinīvijayottaratantram; II; V23

> "A light bug shines only for himself, jewels shine not only for themselves but for a few others also, the stars shine for even more, the moon shines for still more, and the sun shines for the whole universe. In the same way, he who is established in the *śāmbhavopāya* state shines like the midday sun for the whole universe."

As the light bug has sufficient light to show his own body, there are those *yogins* that are sufficient only for themselves; they cannot help anybody else. There are also *yogins*, who like jewels, shine so that their light illumines those that are near. Those *yogins* that shine like stars illuminate even more with their light. Those that shine like the moon illumine still more. But the Śaivaite *yogī*, established in *śāmbhavopāya*, is just like the sun—he lights the whole universe.

Śāktopāya

Śāktopāya is that *upāya* which functions by the means of energies. *Śāktopāya* is called *jñānopāya,* because it is the means which originates from *jñāna śakti*, the energy of knowledge. Here, the aspirant is more important than the Master because he must make himself capable of receiving the Master's grace. He must work to develop great velocity of awareness until he reaches the "feet of the Master." By this I do not mean the Master's physical feet. "Being at the feet of the Master" means reaching that state where the aspirant is capable of receiving the grace of the Master. Those who reach that state are said to be at the feet of the Master.

In *śāktopāya*, the *yogī* does not have to recite *mantras* or use his breath to be aware or concentrate on any particular spot. He has only to see and concentrate on that Supreme Being that is found in two actions without actions. In the "Vijñāna Bhairava Tantra," this is called centering.[2]

In *śāktopāya,* centering can be practiced between any and all actions and or thoughts. In centering, the *yogī* must develop great velocity of awareness. Great velocity means firmness of awareness. Awareness must not become loose. If the *yogī's* awareness becomes loose, he will be forced out of *śāktopāya* into the lowest *upāya*, *āṇavopāya*. He will lose the right to tread on the path of *śāktopāya*. In his practice, there must be continuity in the cycle of his awareness. Only by maintaining an unbroken chain of awareness will he be able to discover the reality between any two thoughts or actions. The practice of centering is meant to function between any two actions or any two thoughts. He can center between any two thoughts or any two movements, between one thought and another thought, between waking and dreaming, between one step and the next step, between one breath and the next breath. All actions and all thoughts are the proper framework for the practice of *śāktopāya*. The *śāktopāya yogī* must simply insert continuous awareness in the center of any two actions or thoughts. If his awareness is faulty and is not unbroken, then he falls and enters into the lowest *upāya*, *āṇavopāya*.

Āṇavopāya

Āṇavopāya is concerned with *aṇu*, the individual soul. *Āṇavopāya* is that *upāya*, which functions by the process of concentrating on *uccāra* (breathing), *karaṇa* (organs of sensa-

2 "madhyaṁ samāśrayet."
Vijñāna Bhairava Tantra; Verse 61

tion), *dhyāna* (contemplation), and *sthāna prakalpanā* (concentrating on a particular place).

The word *uccāra* means "breathing," actually concentration on the breath. Concentration on the breath is the essential element of the practice of *cakrodaya*. In practicing *cakrodaya* you have to continue breathing deeply and find the point, the center between the two breaths, the incoming breath and the outgoing breath. This is the ending point, the beginning point, and also the center of the span of the breath. In *cakrodaya*, however, the beginning and ending points of the span of the breath are predominant. This is *uccāra*, concentration on the breath. It can be either with sound or without sound.

Karaṇa means "organ" and, in particular, it means "sense organ." Concentrating on *karaṇa* means having and maintaining one-pointedness through vision or any other sense organ. In *karaṇa,* the sense of sight is predominant. For example, in concentrating on *karaṇa* through the sense of sight, you have to look at a particular thing. You must go on looking without blinking your eyes. You should go on seeing that one point with unbroken awareness. And when that point vanishes, and it should and will vanish when you enter into that vastness of the center, that is the end. If you were to practice concentrating on *karaṇa* through the sense of hearing, then you would listen to some sound and continue listening and repeat that sound again and again. You can also practice by concentrating on some taste or some particular sensation of touch. In *karaṇa,* you can employ all the five organs of sensation, however; with the senses other than sight, you must remain aware of where the sensation first arises. This is the way of *karaṇa* in *āṇavopāya* and, in the long run, this creates one-pointedness.

The word *dhyāna* means "contemplation." It is another mode in *āṇavopāya*. *Dhyāna* is contemplation on some point. There are different forms of *dhyāna*. For example, you are practicing *dhyāna* when you contemplate on the lotus in your heart, or on the meaning of some *mantra*[3] such as the *mantra* "*so'ham*" or the *mantra* "*śiva*." This is a higher form of *āṇavopāya* because it is contemplation without any shape, without any form. If you were to contemplate on Lord Śiva as having a particular form, a particular shape, that is a lower form of *āṇavopāya*. It is contemplation with form.

Therefore, any time in meditation that you have *mantra,* then you have *dhyāna*. And along with *dhyāna,* you can also adjust *karaṇa* and *uccāra*, but not in the beginning.

Sthāna prakalpanā means concentration on some particular place. The higher form of *sthāna prakalpanā*, which is a practice in higher *āṇavopāya*, is that practice where you discover where each aspect of reality is found in the span of the breath. You see where the *devas* are residing, where the *lokapālas* are residing, where is the location of dawn, where is the location of morning, where is the location of midday, where is the location of sunset (*sandhyā*), where is the location of midnight, where is that location which is the time when the sun moves toward the northern side, and where is that location which is the time when the sun moves to the south. These are all *sthāna prakalpanā*, and these are the particular points you have to concentrate on, and discover in the course of your breath.[4] The practice of *sthāna prakalpanā* is simply to see the vastness of the universe in one breath.

The second and lower form of *sthāna prakalpanā*, which is a practice in lower *āṇavopāya*, is where you concentrate on dif-

---

3 All *mantras* have meaning.

4 In the practice of *sthāna prakalpanā,* there are points in the breath which you must concentrate on. In the practice of *uccāra,* there is no need to concentrate on each and every point in the passage of the breath. In this practice, you concentrate on only one point.

ferent points in the body. These particular places for concentration are divided into three. One place for concentration is between the two eyebrows (*bhrūmadhya*). The second place for concentration is the pit of the throat (*kaṇṭha kūpa*). And the third place of concentration is the heart (*hṛidaya*).

All of these processes, *uccāra*, *karaṇa*, *dhyāna*, and *sthāna prakalpanā*, are called the *upāyas* of *jīva*, the means of the individual, and they exist in *āṇavopāya*.

Āṇavopāya is the means found in the world of duality and is known as *bhedopāya*. The means which exists in the world of mono-duality, in the world where duality and nonduality exist together, is *śāktopāya* and is called *bhedābhedopāya*. That means which exists in the world of pure monism (*abheda*) is *śāmbhavopāya* and is called *abhedopāya*.

Śāmbhavopāya is also called *icchopāya,* as it is the means which exists in *icchā śakti*. The means which exists in *jñāna śakti* is *śāktopāya* and is called *jñānopāya*. *Āṇavopāya* is called *kriyopāya* because it is the means which is found in *kriyā śakti*.

The difference between *āṇavopāya*, *śāktopāya*, and *śāmbhavopāya* is this. In *āṇavopāya,* the strength of your awareness is such that you have to take the support of everything as an aid to maintaining and strengthening your awareness. Though you concentrate on the center, you must take the support of two things for concentrating on that center. In *śāktopāya,* your awareness is strengthened to the extent that only one point is needed as a support for your concentration and that point is the center. In *śāktopāya,* you begin with the center and then become established there. In *śāmbhavopāya,* the strength of your awareness is such that no support is needed. You are already residing in the meant. There is nowhere to go, just reside at your own point. The rest is automatic.

It is important to realize that though there are different *upāyas*, they all lead you to the state of one transcendental consciousness. The difference in these *upāyas* is that *āṇavopāya* will carry you in a long way, *śāktopāya* in a shorter way, and *śāmbhavopāya* in the shortest way. Although the ways are different, the point to be achieved is one.

Anupāya

Beyond these three *upāyas*, *śāmbhavopāya*, *śāktopāya*, and *āṇavopāya*, there is another *upāya*. Although it is not actually an *upāya*, yet it is mentioned in Kashmir Śaivism. This *upāya* is called *anupāya*. The word *anupāya* means "no *upāya*." Thoughtlessness is called *śāmbhavopāya*. One-pointedness is called *śāktopāya*. Concentration on and with the support of *mantra* and breathing and all other elements is called *āṇavopāya*. Above all of these is *anupāya*. In *anupāya,* the aspirant has only to observe that nothing is to be done. Be as you are. If you are talking, go on talking. If you are sitting, go on sitting. Do not do anything, only reside in your being. This is the nature of *anupāya*. *Anupāya* is attributed to *ānanda śakti* of Śiva and is also called *ānandopāya*.

Chapter Six

The Theory of Speech
Vāk

When the aspirant resides in the *śāmbhava* state, in complete universal I-ness (*pūrṇāhantā*), he is traveling in the kingdom of *vāk*, "speech." Here, he resides in the principal and supreme speech which is called *parāvāk*. And not only does this aspirant reside in that state of *parāvāk*, but he travels in other sounds also. He comes out and he goes in. He has the ability of traveling from the supreme to the gross and from the gross to the supreme. He can ascend and descend without varying his consciousness. His consciousness will remain the same in each and every state.

The word *parā* means "supreme," and *parā vāk* is the "supreme speech." It is that soundless sound which resides in your own universal consciousness. It is the supreme sound which has no sound. It is the life of the other three kinds of speech which comprise the kingdom of speech, *paśyantī*, *madhyamā*, and *vaikharī*, and yet it is not in this kingdom of speech. The aspirant's purpose in the kingdom of speech is to travel from *paśyantī* to *madhyamā* and then to *vaikharī*. In your journey you do not travel to *parā* because *parā* is supreme.

Paśyantī vāk is that speech which is without differentiation (*nirvikalpa*). Take, for example, the perception of some object such as a watch. When you look at this watch, you feel that it is a watch. But do not go that far in your perceiving. You have to see something more, what you saw before you felt that it was a watch. Before that, you observed something white, not a watch, only something white. This is that state which is partially undifferentiated (*nirvikalpa*) and partially differentiated (*vikalpa*). This is moving to the first flow of the perception of that which you are observing. At this point in your perception, you see only a white shade. Go still further forward in your perception. You will see that there is some sensation of seeing. You will not see anything. This is *paśyantī vāk*. In this first flow of your perceiving, you were observing, you were looking, but you were not seeing anything. It is only afterwards that you saw a watch. This kind of observation, which takes place at the level of *paśyantī vāk*, is in the *nirvikalpa* state.

Paśyantī vāk is that state where a person is experiencing, observing the world, but not seeing anything. It is only pure sensation without any differentiation (*vikalpa*), without any thought. In our Śaivite literature, the state of *paśyantī vāk* is described as *śikharastha jñāna*. *Śikharastha jñāna* means "knowing something while situated at the top." For example, you climb to the top of a hill and see below a whole town. When you observe that town, you observe it in its entirety. You do not observe it as a collection of separate entities, one by one, such as this is a tree, this is a path, this is a motor car, these are people moving about. Rather, you generally see the town as a whole without differentiation, such as the perception "this is the town of Srinagar," "this is the city of London." And this kind of perception where you perceive something as a whole and not in distinct parts is called *śikharastha jñāna*. This is that seeing which is without thought. You perceive and observe in the same way at the level of *paśyantī vāk.*[1]

The next state of speech (*vāk*) is called *madhyamā vāk. Madhyamā vāk* is between the lowest speech, *vaikharī*, and the highest speech, *paśyantī*. This is the reason that it is called *madhyamā*, speech in the middle state. *Madhyamā vāk* is that state of mind where you reside only in thoughts. This state is only mental. It is without letters, words, or sentences. When you are asleep and dreaming, you are residing in *madhyamā vāk*. Here you are residing only in the mind, not in action and, therefore, you are devoid of sensation.

The third state of speech is called *vaikharī vāk*. The term *vaikharī* means "gross, rough." This gross speech is ordinary speech. When you utilize *vaikharī vāk,* you have to use your tongue and lips.

These three states of speech are, respectively, called subtlest, subtle, and gross. Gross speech is *vaikharī vāk*, subtle speech is *madhyamā vāk*, and subtlest speech is *paśyantī vāk*. Each state of speech is itself also gross (*sthūlā*), subtle (*sūkṣmā*), and subtlest (*parā*). Therefore, there is gross *paśyantī*, subtle *paśyantī*, and subtlest *paśyantī*, gross *madhyamā*, subtle *madhyamā*, and subtlest *madhyamā*, gross *vaikharī*, subtle *vaikharī*, and subtlest *vaikharī*. In Śaivism, the locations of these different refinements of sound are indicated for the easy apprehension of the aspirant.

1 A baby experiences the *nirvikalpa* state, without thought. As the baby grows up, his experiences are both *nirvikalpa* and *savikalpa*. When he becomes old, he only experiences in the *savikalpa* state. Here, in this state of differentiation, he is only barking, "do this, do this, do this." Yet, there is no strength in doing this. In the end, this is a degraded state for individual souls. He has lost the charm of that supremeness. To regain that supremeness, one must gain the *nirvikalpa* state in this *savikalpa* state. It is only then that the *nirvikalpa* state will remain permanently.

First, I will explain gross (*sthūlā*) *paśyantī*, then gross *madhyamā*, and then gross *vaikharī*. Next, I will explain subtle (*sūkṣmā*) *paśyantī*, subtle *madhyamā*, and subtle *vaikharī*. And finally, I will explain subtlest (*parā*) *paśyantī*, subtlest *madhyamā*, and subtlest *vaikharī*.

When you play on any metal-string instrument, such as a *sitāra*, the sound which is produced by that instrument resides in gross *paśyantī*. And when one concentrates on that sound which exists in gross *paśyantī*, one should enter in *samādhi*, enter in that supreme transcendental Being. In fact, it is said in our Kashmir Śaivism, that those who cannot enter into their real nature while listening to the sound of a metal string instrument are worthless. They have no capacity, no ability of concentration. That sound should and must take you inside because that sound is *paśyantī*, even though it is gross *paśyantī*. The sound of gross *madhyamā* is produced by a drum instrument which is covered by leather. Concentration on this gross *madhyamā* is also helpful for carrying the aspirant inside his own real nature.[2]

The third speech, gross *vaikharī*, is said to be all the sounds which are produced by the mouth, through the contact of the lips and tongue. In this state of speech, no concentration is possible. No one can enter into *samādhi* by concentrating on this gross *vaikharī* except for that aspirant who is residing in the *śāmbhava* state. He enters into *samādhi* through ordinary talk. This, therefore, also leads him to that supreme consciousness.

To explain subtle (*sūkṣmā*) *paśyantī*, subtle *madhyamā*, and subtle *vaikharī*, I will combine them and explain them togeth-

2 Although it is easier to enter into gross *paśyantī* than it is to enter into gross *madhyamā*, it is more difficult to reside in gross *paśyantī* than it is to reside in gross *madhyamā*. You can not easily reside in gross *paśyantī* unless you have the grace of the Master.

er, as is traditionally done in our Śaivism.[3] The inclination in thought that (*ṣaḍajaṁ karomi*) "I will play this string instrument," or the inclination (*madhuraṁ vādayāmi*) "I will play on this drum," or the inclination (*bruve vacaḥ*) "I will speak to you," is subtle. It is this thought which resides in the mind, in the consciousness, of the thinker. And this is not so much a thought as an inclination to think this thought. It is that point, that inclination, that first comes to the mind. In these three inclinations to think a thought, the inclination "I will play this string instrument" is subtle *paśyantī*, the inclination "I will play this drum" is subtle *madhyamā*, and the inclination "I will speak to you" is subtle *vaikharī*.

And when only the sensation of the thought "I will play this string instrument," or "I will play this drum," or "I will speak to you," begins, when it just starts to take rise, that sensation, which is only in the thoughtless world, is subtlest. It is before desire.

For those aspirants who reside in the *śāmbhava* state, there are no restrictions of only traveling in some particular *vāk*. They can travel in each and every state of *vāk*, and yet remain in the *śāmbhava* state. The aspirant of the *śāmbhava* state can travel in gross *paśyantī*, subtle *paśyantī*, and subtlest *paśyantī*, gross *madhyamā*, subtle *madhyamā*, and subtlest *madhyamā*, gross *vaikharī*, subtle *vaikharī*, and subtlest *vaikharī*, and still remain in his transcendental state. This is the greatness of the *śāmbhava* state.

The aspirant of the *śākta* state, which is that aspirant who has gained transcendental consciousness through adopting the means of *śāktopāya*, for him there are only two movements of

3 Abhinavagupta explains these three states of subtle sound together in the third chapter of the Tantrāloka.

speech in which he can travel, subtle and subtlest. If he tries to travel in the movement of gross speech, he will be scattered; he will go astray from his reality.

Those aspirants who are in the state of *āṇavopāya* can only utilize the gross movement of speech, because they have no experience of the subtle or the subtlest states of speech. They must, therefore, initially practice on the gross state of speech. In the long run, their concentration on that gross speech will finally carry them to *śāktopāya,* where they will then reside in their own nature.

Chapter Seven

The Three Impurities
Malas

In our Śaiva system, there are three *malas* or impurities. These *malas* reside in *māyā*. They do not reside in *svātantrya śakti*. Even though *svātantrya śakti* and *māyā* are one, yet they are different in the sense that *svātantrya śakti* is that state of energy which can produce the power of going down and coming up again, both at will, whereas *māyā* will only give you the strength of going down and not the ability of rising up again. Once you have come down, you cannot move up again. This is the reality of the state of *māyā*. It binds you.

Māyā śakti is that universal energy which is owned by the individual being, the individual soul. And when that same universal energy is owned by the universal being, it is called *svātantrya śakti*. *Svātantrya śakti* is pure universal energy. Impure universal energy is *māyā*. It is only the formation that changes through a difference of vision. When you experience *svātantrya śakti* in a crooked way, it becomes *māyā śakti* for you. And when you realize that same *māyā śakti* in Reality, then that *māyā śakti* becomes *svātantrya śakti* for you. Therefore, *svātantrya śakti* and *māyā śakti* are actually only one and the three impurities (*malas*), which are to be explained here, reside in *māyā śakti*, not in *svātantrya śakti*.

The three impurities (*malas*) are gross (*sthūla*), subtle (*sūkṣma*), and subtlest (*para*). The gross impurity is called *kārmamala*. It is connected with actions. It is that impurity which inserts impressions, such as those which are expressed in the statements, "I am happy, I am not well, I have pain, I am a great man, I am really lucky", in the consciousness of the individual being. This impurity of action (*kārmamala*) is *śubhāśubhavāsanā*, the impressions of pleasure and pain. And these impressions of pleasure and pain actually remain in your individual consciousness.[1]

The next impurity is called *māyīya mala*. This impurity creates differentiation in one's own consciousness. It is the impurity of ignorance (*avidyā*), the subtle impurity. The thoughts, "This house is mine, that house is not mine; This man is my friend, that man is my enemy; She is my wife, she is not my wife," are all created by *māyīya mala*. *Māyīya mala* creates duality. *Māyīya mala* is *bhinnavedyaprathā*, the feeling that I and others are different. You feel that what you have is different from what others have, that some things are yours and other things are not yours. This is the impurity which makes Lord Śiva appear as many rather than as one.

The third impurity is called *āṇavamala*. It is the subtlest impurity. *Āṇavamala* is the particular internal impurity of the individual. Although he reaches the nearest state of the consciousness of *Śiva*, he has no ability to catch hold of that state. That inability is the creation of *āṇavamala*. For example, if you are conscious of your own nature and then that consciousness

1 An aspirant who resides in the highest state, *anupāya*, or in the *śāmbhava* state would have no *malas*. If he were to hurt himself, he would not feel pain in the way a bound and limited individual would. Instead, he would feel a sensation of consciousness. And yet he would not be attached to that sensation. It would take him in, into his own Being.

fades away and fades away quickly, this fading is caused by *āṇavamala*.

Āṇavamala is *apūrṇatā*, non-fullness. It is the feeling of being incomplete. Due to this impurity, you feel incomplete in every way. Because of this feeling, you create *abhilāṣā*, the desire for completion. As you feel that you are not complete, you desire to become complete. For example, if I have the desire for some particular thing, then it means that I feel that I do not have this thing. This feeling, that you do not have this thing, is caused by *āṇavamala*.

Though you feel incomplete, knowing that there is some lack in you, yet you do not know what this lack really is. You want to hold everything, and yet no matter what you hold, you do not fill your sense of lacking, your gap. You cannot fill this lacking unless the Master points it out to you and then carries you to that point.

Of these three impurities, *āṇavamala* and *māyīya mala* are not in action; they are only in perception, in experience. It is *kārma mala* which is in action.

Chapter Eight

The Seven States of the Seven Perceivers *Pramātṛin*

Now, let us discuss the seven states of the seven *pramātṛins* (perceivers) and their importance. The first state is called *sakala*. The *sakala* state is that state where perception takes place in the objective world and not in the subjective world. In other words, I would call this state the state of *prameya*, the state of the object of perception. It is realized by its *pramātṛi*—the observer who resides in this state, in the field of objectivity and its world.

The second state is called *pralayākala*. This is the state of negation, where the whole world is negated. And the one who resides in this world of negation is called *pralayākala pramātṛi*, the observer of the *pralayākala* state. And this *pramātṛi*, this perceiver, does not experience the state of this voidness because it is actually the state of unawareness. This state would be observed at the time of *mūrcchā*, when one becomes comatose, which is like unnatural and heavy sleep, like deep sleep devoid of dreams. And the observer, *pralayākala pramātṛi*, resides in that void unawareness.

These two states function in the state of individuality, not in the state of your real nature. These are states of worldly people, not spiritual aspirants.

The third state is called *vijñānākala* and the perceiver of this state is called *vijñānākala pramātṛi*. This state is experienced by those who are on the path of *yoga*. Here the *yogī* experiences awareness at times but this awareness is not active awareness, and at other times his awareness is active but he is not aware of that active awareness.[1] This *vijñānākala pramātṛi*, therefore, takes place in two ways: sometimes it is full of action (*svātantrya*) without awareness and sometimes it is full of awareness without action.[2]

In the first state, the state of *sakala pramātṛi*, all the three *malas—āṇava*, *māyīya*, and *kārma mala*—are active. In the second state, the state of *pralayākala pramātṛi*, *kārma mala* is gone and only two *malas* remain, *āṇava mala* and *māyīya mala*. These two *malas* are concerned with thought rather than action, whereas *kārma mala* is concerned with action. In the third state of perceivers the state of *vijñānākala pramātṛi*, only one *mala*, *āṇava mala*, remains while the other two *malas*, *māyīya mala* and *kārma mala*, have ceased functioning.

---

1 svātantryāhānirbodhasya svātantrasyāpyabodhatā
(dvidhāṇavaṁ malamidaṁ svasvarūpāpahānitaḥ)
Īśvarapratyābhijñā Kārikā III;2:4

"*Āṇava mala* is twofold. It is the cause of the ignorance of free will and it is also the cause of the loss of free will. Thus, it carries one away from their own Real Self."

2 Being full of awareness is *jñānapūrṇa*, full of knowledge. Being full of action is *svātantrya*, full of absolute independence.

The fourth state of the observer is called *śuddhavidyā* and its observer is called *mantra*[3] *pramātṛi*. In this state, the observer is always aware with *svātantrya*. All the *malas* have been removed and its observer observes only the state of his own Self, his own Real nature, full of consciousness, full of bliss, full of independent will, full of knowledge, and full of action. Hence, this state, though it is not a stable state, is the real state of *Śiva*. The *mantra* for this state is *ahaṁ ahaṁ*, *idaṁ idaṁ*. The meaning of the first section of this *mantra*, *ahaṁ ahaṁ*, is that in this state the *yogī* experiences that he is the reality, the Real nature of Self, the Truth of this whole universe. The meaning of the second section of this mantra, *idaṁ idaṁ*, tells us, on the other hand, that he also experiences that this universe is false, that it is unreal. Because this state is not stable, the *yogī* does not always remain in this state. The experience comes and goes. Sometimes he experiences this state and sometimes he does not experience it. Sometimes he experiences only *ahaṁ ahaṁ*. Sometimes, when his consciousness is a little damaged, he experiences only *idaṁ idaṁ*. Therefore, his reality of Self remains unstable and uncertain.

The next state is called *īśvara* and its observer is called *mantreśvara pramātṛi*. The word *mantreśvara* means "the one who has sovereignty on *mantra* (*ahaṁ*–I)." This state is like that of *mantra pramātṛi*, full of consciousness, full of bliss, full of will, full of knowledge, and full of action; however, this is a

---

3 The meaning of the word *mantra*, in the sense that it is being used here, is found in the roots which comprise it, *manana* and *trāṇa*. *Manana* means "awareness, possessing complete knowledge." *Trāṇa* means "complete protection, protection from all the four sides, that protection which protects the whole ignorant world from ignorance." Therefore, *mantra* is that knowledge by which we are protected.

more stable state. The aspirant finds more stability here. The *mantra* for this state is *idaṁ ahaṁ*. The meaning of this *mantra* is that the aspirant feels that this whole universe is not false; on the contrary, he feels that this whole universe is the expansion of his own nature. In the state of *mantra pramātṛi,* he felt that the universe was false, that he was the truth of this reality. Now he unites the state of the universe with the state of his own consciousness. This is actually the unification of *jīva*, the individual, with *Śiva*, the universal.

The next state is the state of *sadāśiva*. The observer of this state is called *mantra maheśvara*. In this state, the observer finds himself to be absolutely one with the Universal Transcendental Being. He experiences this state to be more valid, more solid and deserving of confidence. Once he enters into this state, there is no question at all of falling from it. This is the established state of his Self, his own Real nature. The *mantra* of this state is *ahaṁ idaṁ*. The meaning of this *mantra* is, "I am this universe." Here, he finds his Self in the universe, while in the previous state of *mantreśvara* he found the universe in his Self. This is the difference.

The seventh and last state is the state of Śiva and the observer of this state is no other than *Śiva* Himself. In the other six, the state is one thing and the observer is something else. In this final state, the state is *Śiva* and the observer is also *Śiva*. There is nothing outside *Śiva*. The *mantra* in this state is *ahaṁ*, universal I. Thisness is gone, melted in His I-ness. This state is completely filled with consciousness, bliss, will, knowledge, and action.

The reader must know that in these seven states of seven *pramātṛins,* there are seven *pramātṛi śaktis*. These are the energies of the seven *pramātṛins*. The first energy, by which one is capable of residing in all the three *malas* and thereby remaining in the state of *sakala,* is called *sakala pramātṛi śakti*. The second energy is that energy which makes one capable of residing in unawareness, in voidness (*śūnya*). This energy is called *pralayākala pramātṛi śakti*. That energy which enables one to be seated in the state of *vijñānākala*, where only *āṇava mala* is active, is called *vijñānākala pramātṛi śakti*. The fourth energy, which makes it possible for one to reside in the state of *ahaṁ ahaṁ, idaṁ idaṁ* in the state of *mantrapramātṛi*, which is the state of *śuddhavidyā*, is called *mantra pramātṛi śakti*. In this state, all of the *malas* have vanished completely. The fifth energy is that energy which carries you in the state of *mantreśvara* and is called *mantreśvara pramātṛi śakti*. This is the energy which is found in the state of *īśvara*. The sixth energy is that energy which conveys the *yogī* to the state of *sadāśiva*, the state of *mantra maheśvara*. This energy is called *mantra maheśvara śakti* and it carries the aspirant in the perception of *ahaṁ idaṁ,* where he finds his I-ness in the universe. The seventh energy is the state of that energy of *Śiva*. This energy strengthens the state which is already established in the state of Supreme I-ness, the state of the universal and transcendental "I." This energy is called *śiva pramātṛi śakti*.

It is for this reason that in the *Mālinī Vijaya Tantram* the purpose of these seven states is fully described for the benefit of the aspirant. This description is called *pañcadaśavidhiḥ*, the mode of fifteen-fold thought for rising and returning, for ascending and descending. This means that the theory of the seven *pramātṛins* and their seven energies is meant not only for rising but also for descending. The aspirant must be capable of both rising and descending. The one who rises and cannot descend is incomplete. It is that aspirant who can rise and also descend simultaneously who is considered to be complete and full.

So, in conclusion, the state of *Śiva* is actually that state where *Śiva* can rise and descend, and after descending, can rise again. On the other hand, the state of individuality is that state where *Śiva* descends from the state of Śiva to the state of individuality and then, having descended, cannot rise again. This is the difference between the reality of Śiva and the reality of individual.

Chapter Nine

The Seven Processes of the Seven Perceivers *Pramātṛin*

In considering the seven states of the seven *pramātṛins*, it is important for you to know where these different states exist. The state of *sakala* is found to be existing from *pṛithvī tattva*, the element earth, to *puruṣa tattva*. That is, all of the *tattvas* existing from *pṛithvī tattva*, up to and including *puruṣa tattva*, are established in the *sakala pramātṛi* state. The *pralayākala* state is found to be existing in *māyā tattva*. *Māyā tattva* is simply voidness, a gap. Contained in *māyā tattva* are the two *malas*, *āṇava mala* and *māyīya mala*. In *māyā tattva, kārma mala* is subsided, existing at this point only in seed form. Therefore, in the state of *pralayākala*, one *mala*, *kārma mala*, has become inactive and, from the experiencer's point of view, has disappeared. *Āṇava* and *māyīya mala*, however, remain and are active.

Between *māyā tattva* and *śuddhavidyā tattva*, there is a large gap which has not been included in the class of the *tattvas*. This semi *tattva* is called *mahāmāyā tattva*, even though it is not actually a *tattva*. This *tattva* causes only dissolution, going down and down. In *mahāmāyā tattva* is found the existence of *vijñānākala*.

In *śuddhavidyā tattva,* you find the state of *mantra pramātā,* which is also called *śuddhavidyā pramātṛi.* In *īśvara tattva,* you find the state of *mantreśvara pramātṛi,* which is also called *īśvara pramātā.* And in *sadāśiva tattva,* you will experience the state of *mantra maheśvara pramātṛi.*

In the above six states, you will find that both the state and the state holder, the state and the experiencer of that state, exist together simultaneously. Both shine at the same time. In the seventh state, however, the state of *śiva pramātṛi*, neither the experiencer (*pramātṛi*) nor the object of experience (*prameya*), the state or the state holder, is found separately. Here, *Śiva* is the state and *Śiva* is also the state holder. The observer and the observed are one in the state of *śiva pramātṛi.* Hence, all of the thirty-six *tattvas* are found in the states of the seven *pramātṛins.*

The fifteen-fold process (*pañcadaśavidhiḥ*) teaches us how to rise from the lowest state of objectivity and enter into subjective consciousness. This fifteen-fold process is composed of seven *pramātṛins*, seven *pramātṛi śaktis* (energies) and, fifteenth, the object. In this process, we begin with objectivity in the state of *sakala pramātṛi.* For instance, take any form which is created with the element earth, such as an earthen pot. Look at the pot, just go on looking at it, seeing it. The pot is the object that we are perceiving. This is objectivity in the state of *sakala pramātṛi*. At the time when you are perceiving the pot, you forget the state of observer, the one who is observing this pot. At the time of perceiving the pot, you yourself become the pot. You are completely unaware of your own consciousness. This is the state of *svarūpa*, the fifteenth, complete objectivity. Here the subjective state has merged with the objective state. This is complete objectivity in the *sakala* state. This is the starting point in the fifteen-fold process of rising. It is from here that you must begin, little by little, to develop your awareness. While perceiving the pot, you develop awareness of the perceiver and there you will find the state of *sakala pramātṛi*. The means by which you perceive this state is called *sakala pramātṛi śakti*, the energy of *sakala pramātṛi*.

Then, continuing the fifteen-fold process of rising, you must also rise from this state of *sakala pramātṛi* and enter that state where you are fully aware of yourself as the perceiver. In this state the objective element, the pot, is gone and only you, the perceiver, remain. In this state of the perceiver, in order to continue to rise, you must now also remove the thought of the perceiver. Along with the thought of being the perceiver, in the background, the perceived also exists. When the perceiver exists, the perceived is also to be found in the background, not vividly, but it is there. We must, therefore, also rise from the state of the perceiver. And while rising from the state of the perceiver to the state of the super perceiver, you fall in voidness. This voidness is the state of *pralayākala*[1] *pramātṛi*. This *pralayākala* state is absolutely void.

When you are in the *pralayākala* state, it is almost certain that you will lose consciousness. When you do not lose consciousness of your Being and you are in the *pralayākala* state, then you are in the state of *vijñānākala pramātṛi*.

From the state of *vijñānākala pramātṛi,* you are carried automatically to *mantrapramātṛi,* then to *mantreśvara pramātṛi,* then to *mantramaheśvara pramātṛi,* and, finally, to the state of *Śiva*. You must apply effort only up to the crossing of *māyā*. *Māyā* is the borderline. Once you have crossed *māyā*,

1 The Sanskṛit word *kala* means "sensation." The Sanskṛit word *Sa-kala*, therefore, means "with sensation" and the Sanskṛit word *pralayākala* means the "dissolution" or "absence" of sensation.

which is the state of *pralayākala*, then everything is automatic, everything is solved.[2]

This is the reality of *pañcadaśīvidhiḥ*, the fifteen-fold process of rising. This process can and must be performed in each and every field, the subjective field, the cognitive field, and the objective field, from *pṛithvī tattva*, the element earth, to *puruṣa tattva*. You can perform this process only in *pṛithvī tattva* and all the processes will be complete or you can perform this process on the organs and all the processes will be complete. You can perform this process on any of the *tattvas* from *pṛithvī* to *puruṣa tattva*.

The next process which you must perform is called *trayodaśavidhiḥ*. The Sanskṛit word *trayodaśavidhiḥ* means "thirteen-fold process." The thirteen-fold process includes six *pramātṛins*, six *pramātṛi* energies, and the object. This thirteen-fold process can only be accessed when you have mastered the fifteen-fold process. The object of this thirteen-fold process on which you have to perform and from which you have to rise is *sakala pramātṛi*, including its energy. And the observer in this process is *pralayākala pramātṛi* and the means by which it observes *sakala pramātṛi* is *pralayākala śakti*. First, you have to rise from some being existing in no being. Then you travel. The perceiver must perceive the duality which is individual being in voidness without any thought. And when that perception is no longer voidness, then it will be all consciousness. This is the state of *vijñānākala pramātṛi*. From this state, you rise automatically to *mantra pramātṛi*, *mantreśvara*

---

2 It is the Grace of God which carries you from the lowest point to the highest point. You are automatically carried after you cross the boundary of *māyā*; however, His Grace has been with you throughout the whole of your journey. His Grace is always there in the background for if it were not there you could not do anything.

pramātṛi, *mantra maheśvara pramātṛi*, and finally, to *śiva pramātṛi*. This is the thirteen-fold process as it is explained in the *Mālinī Vijaya Tantra*. This process is meant for highly qualified *yogins*.

The fifteen-fold process and the thirteen-fold process differ in that in the fifteen-fold process you have to rise from objectivity to Universal Being, whereas in the thirteen-fold process, you have nothing to do with the objective world. In the thirteen-fold process, you have to rise from individuality, from individual being, to Universal Being. In the fifteen-fold process, once you have attained the state of Universal Being, the process is complete and you then have to step up to the thirteen-fold process.

After you have completed the thirteen-fold process, then you must begin *ekādaśavidhiḥ*, the eleven-fold process. The eleven-fold process includes five *pramātṛins*, five *pramātṛi* energies and the object from which you have to rise. In this process the object is the state of *pralayākala pramātṛi*, complete and utter voidness. In this process then, you have to rise from voidness. When you have the capacity to rise from voidness, you are greater. You must be very subtle to be able to rise from voidness. It is absolutely impossible for *sakala pramātṛi* to rise from voidness. It is easy to rise from objectivity or from subtle things, but it is extremely difficult to rise from voidness.

Even though you have attained Universal Being in the fifteen-fold process of rising, you do not have the capacity to maintain that universal state. The purpose of functioning these increasingly difficult processes is to strengthen your capacity of rising so that you can maintain this capacity and never fall from the state of Universal Being.

When, in the eleven-fold process, you make *pralayākala pramātṛi* the object and starting point of this process, then the perceiver will be *vijñānākala pramātṛi*. He will automatically travel from *vijñānākala pramātṛi* to *mantra pramātṛi*, *mantreś-*

vara pramātṛi, *mantra maheśvara pramātṛi*, and finally, to *śiva pramātṛi*.

After completing the eleven-fold process you must begin *navātmaviddhiḥ*, the nine-fold process. This process includes four *pramātṛins*, four *pramātṛi* energies, and the object. In this process *vijñānākala pramātṛi* is the object and the perceiver is *mantra pramātṛi*. From *mantra pramātṛi,* rising will take place automatically and you will rise to *mantreśvara pramātṛi, mantra maheśvara pramātṛi*, and *śiva pramātṛi*. This process is completely automatic, nothing is to be done. In all of the earlier processes, the fifteen-fold process, the thirteen-fold process, and even in the eleven-fold process, *māyā* to a greater or lesser extent is present. In the ninefold process, *māyā* has completely disappeared. This and the following processes have only to be done once. They are completely automatic. They are done only to strengthen your awareness. You want your awareness to be absolutely strengthened when you reach the state of *Śiva*.

After completing this ninefold process, you must begin *saptatattvātmaviddhiḥ*, the sevenfold process. This includes three *pramātṛins*, three *pramātṛi śaktis*, and the object. The object in this process is *mantra pramātṛi* (*śuddhavidyā*) and the observer is *mantreśvara*. You will automatically travel from the *mantreśvara* state to *mantra maheśvara* and then to *śiva pramātṛi*.

Next, you must take up *pañcatattvātmavidhiḥ*, the fivefold process. Here, there are two *pramātṛins*, two *pramātṛi śaktis*, and the object. The object here is *mantreśvara* (*īśvara*) and the perceiver is *mantra maheśvara pramātṛi*. Here, you travel automatically from *mantra maheśvara pramātṛi* to *śiva pramātṛi*.

The final process which you must undergo is *tritattvātmavidhiḥ*, the threefold process. The object in this process is *mantra maheśvara pramātṛi* (*sadāśiva*). Here, the perceiver and the energy of perception is only one and that is *Śiva*. This is the last process because here there is only one objective being and one subjective being. *Śadāśiva* is the object and the perceiver is *Śiva*. "*Śiva sākṣāt na bhidyate,*" "Upon realizing *Śiva*, no other process remains." There is no onefold process. When you perceive the state of *sadāśiva* as the object, you are in the state of *Śiva*. No more rising can take place. There is nowhere to rise to. You automatically become that One Universal Being seated in that state of *Śiva* as observed and as observer. Here, you rise from *Śiva* to *Śiva*, from transcendental being to transcendental being. This state is completely full. Here, thisness is found in *Śiva* and *Śiva* is found in thisness. It is said

> abhedebhedanaṁ bhedite ca
> antarānusaṁdhānena abhedanam /

> "See duality in unity and unity in duality."

This is the actual state of Śaivism wherein you realize that the point from which you have to start is the ending point, that the existence of *Śiva* is the same at the starting point and at the ending point. There is really nowhere to go and nothing to be done. It is for the obtaining of this reality of Universal Oneness that we are taught *pañcadaśavidhiḥ*, the fifteen-fold process, in the *Mālinī Vijaya Tantra*.

Chapter Ten

The Five Great Acts of Lord Śiva *Pañcakṛityavidhiḥ* including His *Grace (Śaktipāta)*

The five great acts of Lord Śiva are *sṛiṣṭi*, the creative act; *sthiti*, the protective act; *saṁhāra*, the destructive act; *tirodhāna*, the act of enfolding or concealing His nature; and *anugraha*, the act of unfolding or revealing His nature. Each of these acts is also accomplished by the individual soul. In the case of the individual, however, they are not called acts, but "actions," because this kind of act is dependent on the will of God, not on the will of the individual being. The individual being does not act according to his own will; he cannot. He is dependent on the will of God, Lord Śiva. It is only God that is completely independent. There is a difference, therefore, between "action" and "act." Action is attributed to the individual soul and act is attributed to Lord Śiva.

If you believe that because the individual soul does not perform acts but only actions, and that he has no freedom and, therefore, cannot be held responsible for his actions, you are wrong. The limited individual is responsible for his actions. He does have ego and feels that he is acting himself. When he feels that he is acting himself, then he is responsible for his actions. If he were to feel that Lord Śiva is really the actor and that it is

Lord Śiva acting, not himself, only then is he not responsible for his actions. But then, of course, he could do no wrong.

In the kingdom of spirituality, Lord Śiva creates masters and disciples through His fifth act, the act of grace (*anugraha*). This grace is ninefold and, therefore, He creates masters and disciples in nine different ways.

The first and highest level of grace is called *tīvratīvra śaktipāta*. *Tīvratīvra śaktipāta* means "super supreme grace." When Lord Śiva bestows super supreme grace on anyone, then that person becomes perfectly self-recognized. He knows his real nature completely and in perfection. At the same time, however, this kind of intense grace can not be resisted by his body, so he throws away his body and dies. This person becomes a master; however, he accomplishes the act of his mastery secretly in the deserving hearts of disciples. He is not visible in this world. Only those who are deserving experience his subtle existence.

The second intensity of grace is called *tīvramadhya śaktipāta*. This is "supreme medium grace." The effect of this grace of Lord Śiva is that the recipient becomes completely and perfectly illumined, but does not leave his body. He is said to be a *prātibha guru*, that is, a master who is made not by another master's initiation, but by his self, by his own grace. He experiences spontaneous enlightenment. These particular masters live in this world with their physical bodies for the upliftment of mankind.

The third intensity of grace is called *tīvramanda śaktipāta,* which means "inferior supreme grace." In one who has received this grace the desire appears for going to the feet of a spiritual master. And the master that he finds has received the second intensity of grace, *tīvramadhya śaktipāta*. This master is perfect. He is all knowing. There is no difference between this master and Śiva. The master does not initiate him, rather, he simply touches him with his divine hand, or gazes upon him, or embraces him, and at that very moment this disciple, who is a recipient of medium supreme grace, perfectly transcends individuality and enters into that supreme transcendental state without the need of practicing *japa* (recitation) or *dhyāna* (contemplation), etc. Although he still experiences pleasure and pain in his physical body, it does not affect him, as his being has become supreme.

That master who has received this particular intensity of grace, which is known as *Rudra śakti-samāveśaḥ,* is called *Rudra śakti-samāviṣṭaḥ* because he has completely entered into the trance of *Rudra śakti*, the energy of *Śiva*. He exhibits five signs which can be observed by others. The first sign is his intense love for Lord Śiva. The second sign is that whenever he recites any *mantra,* the *devatā* (deity) of that *mantra* appears to him at once without his having to wait. This is called *mantrasiddhiḥ*. The third sign which can be observed is that he has control over the five elements. The fourth sign is that whatever work he begins, he completes that work without defect. And the fifth sign is that either he is a master of all the scriptures or he becomes a great poet.

Lord Śiva, through these three supreme intensities of grace, creates masters in the kingdom of spirituality. With lower intensities of grace Lord Śiva creates worthy disciples.

The fourth intensity of grace is called *madhyatīvara śaktipāta*. This is "medium supreme grace." Through the effect of this intensity of grace, the disciple reaches the feet of that master who is absolutely perfect. But because the foundation established in the mind of this disciple is not quite completely perfect, the mere touch or glance of this perfect master will not bring this disciple to enlightenment. He, therefore, initiates this disciple in the proper fashion by giving him a *mantra* and teaching him the proper way of treading. Through this initiation, the disciple becomes enlightened but during the period of the existence of his physical body, he is not completely satisfied with this enlightenment. When he leaves his physical body at the time of his death, however, he obtains completely satisfactory results from the initiation he had received earlier and becomes one with *Śiva*.

The fifth intensity of grace is called *madhyamadhya śaktipāta,* which means "medium middle grace." When Lord Śiva bestows this particular intensity of grace upon someone, the intense desire for achieving the existence of Lord Śiva arises in this person's mind. At the same time, however, he does not want to ignore the enjoyments of the world. He wants to enjoy worldly pleasures along with wanting to realize the existence of Lord Śiva. Yet the intensity of his desire is only for achieving Lord Śiva's state. So, although he is initiated by a master and realizes his real nature as Lord Śiva, his real self, and enjoys the bliss of that state while remaining in his physical body, simultaneously he also enjoys the pleasures of the world. But as these worldly pleasures, which take place in this mortal field of the universe, are not real pleasures, at the time of his leaving his physical body, he enters into the kingdom of paradise (*svargaloka*) and enjoys all the worldly pleasures to his entire satisfaction. After he has satisfied his desire for worldly pleasures, he does not come down again into this world but is again initiated by his master, who is all-pervading, while he remains in heaven. Through this initiation, he becomes complete and realizes the reality of his supreme nature and he enters into the kingdom of Lord Śiva and merges in Him completely from heaven itself.

The sixth intensity of grace is called *madhyamanda śaktipāta,* which means "medium inferior grace." The effect of this grace is very much like the effect of medium middle grace; however, the difference lies in predominance. The effect of medium middle grace is that in the mind of the disciple arises both the desire for attaining the state of Lord Śiva and the desire for experiencing worldly pleasures. The predominant desire, however, is for attaining the state of Lord Śiva. The effect of medium inferior grace is also that in the mind of this disciple arise both the desire for attaining the state of Lord Śiva and the desire for experiencing worldly pleasures. However, the predominant desire here is for experiencing worldly pleasures. Though he achieves self-realization, it is not complete because of the agitation he experiences seeking worldly pleasures. So at the time of his leaving his physical body, this intensity of grace carries him from this mortal world first to paradise, where he enjoys the pleasures of the world. But while in paradise he does not gain the fitness to begin practicing for attaining the realization of his self. He must, therefore, be again reborn and come down into this mortal field. And from that very birth he sentences his mind toward the fulfillment of his self-realization. Although his life in this mortal realm is very short, as Lord Śiva wants to carry him quickly to his own state, he becomes absolutely complete in that short span of time and enters, in the end, into the transcendental state of *Śiva*.

The above three medium intensities of grace take place in the field of aspirants living in the kingdom of *Śivadharma*. Those aspirants have the inclination to achieve the state of self-realization at least half hourly during the day and at least twice during the night. The remaining period they keep aside for worldly pleasures.

The following three inferior intensities of grace—*manda tīvra* (inferior supreme), *manda madhya* (inferior medium), and *manda manda* (inferior inferior)—take place in the field of aspirants living in *lokadharmaḥ*, the kingdom of worldly life. These aspirants have the desire for achieving self-realization, the state of Lord Śiva, only when the pains and pressures of this world become too much to bear. At that moment, they want to abandon everything and achieve self-realization but they are not able to, and though they want to leave this worldly life, they cannot. These aspirants have more tendency for worldly pleasure and less tendency for realizing their Self. But, as the grace of Lord Śiva shines in them, in the end, which may take many lifetimes, they become one with the supreme being. This is the greatness of Lord Śiva's grace—that no matter what intensity of His grace is with you, it will carry you to his nature in the end.

Chapter Eleven

The Five States of the Individual Subjective Body

On the path of the thirty-six elements, only one universal subjective body is traveling in each element. There are not unlimited subjects traveling in these elements. All subjects (*jīvas*) are actually only the one subjective body of God. When he travels in the element of earth, he becomes earth and loses his subjectivity of self. When he travels in the element of air, he becomes air and loses his subjectivity of self. And this is the case with all of the thirty-six elements. They are actually only one universal subjective body. This one subjective body travels, therefore, from earth to *Śiva* and when that subjective body reaches the state of *Śiva*, it becomes *Śiva*.

As one universal subjective body travels in the thirty-six elements, the individual subjective body travels in five states. When this individual subjective body travels in objectivity and it becomes the object and ignores its subjective consciousness, this is one state. When it travels in the cognitive world and becomes one with that and loses consciousness of its subjectivity, this is the second state. When it travels in the subjective world without being conscious of that and becomes one with that unconscious subjectivity, this is the third state. When it travels in absolute subjective consciousness and it becomes that subjective consciousness, this is the fourth state. And when it becomes fully established in that subjective consciousness, that is the fifth state. These five states, which comprise the individual subjective body, are called *jāgrat*, wakefulness, *svapna*, dreaming, *suṣupti*, deep sleep, *turya*, the fourth state, and *turyātītā*, beyond the fourth.

In *jāgrat*, wakefulness, the individual subjective body is traveling in the world of objectivity (*prameya*), which comprises the world of elements, names, forms, words, and sounds. Here, it loses consciousness of its subjectivity and becomes one with the objective world. In *svapna*, the dreaming state, the individual subjective body travels in the impressions (*saṁskāras*) of the objective world. Here, it also loses the awareness of its subjective consciousness. It takes hold of these impressions and becomes one with the world of impressions. In *suṣupti*, deep dreamless sleep, it has entered a state of complete void (*śūnya*). If it was previously traveling in the world of objectivity in the waking state, then upon entering deep sleep, it loses consciousness of this objectivity and also of its subjectivity. If it was previously traveling in the world of impressions in the dreaming state, then upon entering deep sleep, it loses consciousness of these impressions. In deep sleep, it is no longer aware of anything. The impressions of the objective world remain but these are as if dead. When it again returns from the state of deep sleep, these impressions, which were seemingly dead, again come to life. And when, by the grace of a master, this subjective body enters into subjective consciousness with full awareness, and maintaining unbroken awareness becomes fully illumined in its own Self, this is called the fourth state, *turya*. And when this individual subjective body takes a firm hold of *turya* and does not lose consciousness for even a moment, then it is established in that state called *turyātītā*, above the fourth. It is completely established in its Self. Its awareness of Self is maintained constantly in wakefulness, dreaming, and deep sleep. It never loses its consciousness. Even at the time of death, because it lives in the body of consciousness, it remains completely Self aware.

Now I will explain to you how the four states of the individual—*jāgrat*, *svapna*, *suṣupti*, and *turya*—are found in each of these four states.[1] First, let us take the state of *jāgrat*, wakefulness, and see how these four exist in the waking state. The first state is *jāgrat jāgrat*, wakefulness in the world of wakefulness. Actually, this objective wakefulness is the absence of wakefulness in the real sense because in this state you are fully given to the world of objectivity and you completely lose consciousness of your subjectivity. This is the state of complete objectivity. People who exist here are totally given to the objective world. They are never conscious of their self. They are absolutely unaware. They never ask the question, "Who am I?" When they observe an object, such as a pot, they become completely one with that object and lose the consciousness that they are observers. In Śaivism we call this state *abuddhaḥ*, the state of absolute unawareness.

The next state is called *jāgrat svapna*, dreaming in the state of wakefulness. When subjective consciousness enters into objective consciousness and then loses awareness of that objectivity and lives only in the impressions of objectivity while in wakefulness, this is dreaming in the state of wakefulness. For instance, when, in the objective world, you look at a particular person and you are not aware of looking at that person, then you are traveling in your own impressions; this is

1 *Turyātitā*, beyond the fourth, is not found mixed with any other state. *Turyātitā* is absolute. In *turyātitā*, there is no contact of either objectivity or subjectivity. It is for this reason that only four different modes are to be found in each of the four states of the individual subjective body. *Turyātitā* is not explained nor is it recognized in this context.

jāgrat svapna. In ordinary worldly life when a person is in the state of *jāgrat svapna,* we say that he is daydreaming or that he is lost in thought. In our philosophy, we call this state *budhāvasthā*, that state which has some awareness, some consciousness.

The next state in *jāgrat* is called *jāgrat suṣupti*, deep sleep in the state of wakefulness. When in the state of wakefulness that individual subjective body, both externally and internally, loses consciousness of the objective world and also loses consciousness of the world of impressions, he is in the state of *jāgrat suṣupti*. Externally, he is not experiencing the objective world and internally, he is not experiencing the world of impressions. In our Śaivism, this state is called *prabuddhaḥ*, "with consciousness," because he has reached very near to the Supreme Consciousness of Being.

The highest and most refined state in *jāgrat* is called *jāgrat turya*, the fourth state in the state of wakefulness. In this state, the individual subjective body, after losing consciousness of both external and internal objectivity, enters into some consciousness of Self, of Being. He is partly illuminated by that awareness of Self and becomes quite aware internally of the consciousness of Self. He moves and travels in the objective world, and at the same time, he resides in Self-Consciousness. He does not lose hold of his internal subjective consciousness. In Śaivism, *jāgrat turya* is called *suprabuddhaḥ*, absolutely full of awareness.

Also in *svapna*, the dreaming state, where you travel only in impressions, the four modes of *jāgrat*, *svapna*, *suṣupti*, and *turya* are to be found. *Svapna* is the state found in dreaming, in impressions, in memory, in madness, and in intoxication. The first state in *svapna* is known as *svapna jāgrat*, wakefulness in the state of dreaming. When the subjective body travels in impressions and is given to those impressions in the field of objectivity and, at the same time, loses consciousness of those impressions, this is the state of individuality called *svapna jāgrat*. Here, this individual sometimes travels in the waves of impressions and sometimes travels in the waves of objectivity. For example, if in a dream you see a pencil and then, when you look again, you see a knife in place of the pencil, you are not conscious of this change. You do not ask the question, "Why is there now a knife where there once was a pencil?" Everything in this state, normal or abnormal, seems normal and ordinary to you. It is objective because you are given to objectivity and are lost in the object, which in this example is the pencil. The question, "How is this so?" does not arise in your mind. This state in Śaivism is called *gatāgatam*, which means "you come and you go," sometimes it is a pencil and sometimes it is not a pencil.

The next state found in *svapna*, the dreaming state, is called *svapna svapna*, dreaming in the state of dreaming. In this state, the individual subjective body travels only in the world of impressions without the least awareness of their connection of one to the other. You see a pencil, then you see a book, then you fly in the air, then you are driving a automobile, and yet you are not aware of any of this. You feel that everything is perfectly okay. In our Śaivism, this state is called *suvikṣiptam*, "absolutely dispersed consciousness." You travel here and there, you do this and that, and yet you do not know anything.

The third state found in *svapna* is called *svapna suṣupti*, "deep sleep in the state of dreaming." Sometimes in the dreaming state, this subjective body, while traveling in the world of impressions and thoughts, also develops some awareness of subjectivity. If, for example, you were to see a pencil in a dream and then in the next moment you were to see a knife in place of the pencil, you would wonder why the pencil has become a knife. You realize that you are not awake, that you must be dreaming. You are traveling in subjectivity; however, that subjectivity does not remain. Because this state is *suṣupti* in the state of dreaming, your subjective consciousness comes and goes. You question and argue and then you forget, you lose this consciousness and are again traveling in impressions. This state of individuality is called *saṁgatam*, which means "touched." Here, you experience the occasional touch of consciousness.

The next and highest state in *svapna* is called *svapna turya*, the fourth state in the state of dreaming. When you are in the dreaming state and observe some particular object, you perceive this particular object in the world of impressions. And when at that very moment, while in the dreaming state, you become aware, you become conscious that you are not awake, that you are in the dreaming state and, by the grace of your master, you cast away the objective world of impressions and enter into *samādhi*, this is the state of *svapna turya*. This state also is not permanent. Again, you fall into the dreaming state full of impressions and begin to dream. Realizing that you are again dreaming, you enter again into *samādhi* and then another dream comes and takes you away. You move from the dreaming state to *samādhi* and back to the dreaming state and again to *samādhi* and so forth. You are incapable of maintaining that state of *samādhi*. This condition is known in Śaivism as *susamāhitam*, which means "absolutely aware, full of awareness."

In the state of *suṣupti*, deep sleep, the first state of these four modes is *suṣupti jāgrat*, wakefulness in the state of deep sleep. In this state, you lose all impressions and thoughts and remain in absolute void (*śūnya*). While remaining in this state, you are not aware and you do not taste its joy. For example, if you have fallen into this state of sound dreamless sleep, where you travel neither in objectivity nor in impressions, and then when you emerge from that dreamless state, someone asks you, "Where were you?" You would reply (*nakiñcidjño'smi*), "I do not know anything." Sometimes upon awakening from deep sleep, you realize that while you were asleep you did not know anything; however, you do know that you were happily sleeping and that it was absolutely peaceful. This experience "I was peacefully sleeping" does not occur in *suṣupti jāgrat*. In the state of *suṣupti jāgrat,* you remember afterwards that you were experiencing nothing.

na kiñcidahamavediṣam
gāḍha mūḍho'hamasvāpsam

"I was asleep and I observed nothing."

In our Śaivism, this state is called *uditaṁ*, "full of rising." It is said to be full of rising because you have thrown away the world of impressions and have entered into the negation of impressions. You are rising out of the world of impressions toward *Śiva*.

The next state in deep sleep is called *suṣupti svapna*, "dreaming in the state of deep sleep." While in deep sleep, you are traveling in the world of unconscious subjectivity. It is the world of subjectivity where subjectivity is absent from consciousness. In deep sleep there is no consciousness, no awareness of subjectivity. You remain in that subjectivity but you do not know that you are in subjectivity. In the state of *suṣupti svapna*, however, you have some impression of being in subjectivity, there is some cognition of remaining there. In this state, you are somewhat conscious that you are traveling in subjectivity. We call this state *vipulam*, which means "gets nourished." This means that the impression and awareness that you are traveling in the world of subjective consciousness gradually becomes stronger and stronger; it slowly increases.

The third state of deep sleep is called *suṣupti suṣupti*, deep sleep in the state of deep sleep. In this state, while you are traveling in the world of subjective consciousness, the impression, the faint idea that this is the world of subjective consciousness, remains in the background throughout, without interruption. In the state of *suṣupti svapna,* you also have some impression of remaining in subjectivity; however, it is an interrupted perception. Yet in both cases, in *suṣupti svapna* and in *suṣupti suṣupti*, where the impression, the faint idea that this is the world of subjective consciousness remains in the background, *suṣupti* is predominant. This state, in which the subtle awareness that this is the world of subjective consciousness remains in uninterrupted continuity, is called in our Śaivism *śāntām. Śāntām* means "peaceful." It is so named because your awareness remains in the background in an absolutely peaceful state. In this state, there is no agitation.

The fourth state of deep sleep is *suṣupti turya*, the fourth mode in the state of deep sleep. In this state, you travel in the world of subjective consciousness. You are continuously aware of that subjective consciousness in the background and at the same time you experience the bliss of this state. In *suṣupti suṣupti,* you do not experience the real bliss of this subjective state, you experience only its peace. Here, in *suṣupti turya*, you experience the positive bliss of this state. Here, you are entering *samādhi* and yet consciousness still remains in the background. We call this state *suprasannā* because this is that state in which you are absolutely full of bliss, even though you are not fully aware of that bliss.[2]

Let's turn now and look again at the three states of the individual subjective body. The word *jāgrat* refers to that state wherein one is full of awareness from his own point of view, from the point of view of individual consciousness, not from

---

2 uditaṁ vipulaṁ śāntaṁ suprasannamathāparam

Mālinī Vijaya Tantra: II;45

the point of view of subjective consciousness. It is worldly people that call this state *jāgrat* (waking). *Yogins*, on the other hand, have a different name for it. *Yogins* feel that when you enter in the state of objective consciousness, you become one with objectivity. This, therefore, is not actually the state of waking. It cannot be *jāgrat*. It is really the state of becoming one with objectivity. For this reason, this state is called *piṇḍasthaḥ,* a state where you become one with whatever you perceive. Enlightened souls (*jñānīs*) have yet another name for it. In this state the Being of Śiva has expanded his body of consciousness in names, forms, space, and time. These *jñānīs* feel the consciousness of Śiva everywhere. It is for this reason that they call this state *sarvatobhadra*[3] which means "everywhere divine." Wherever they go, these enlightened souls feel the divinity of God Consciousness. Whenever they travel in the objective world, whether in name, form, space, time, whether walking or talking, whatever they may be doing, they are traveling in Absolute Consciousness.

The dreaming state is called *svapna* (the absence of worldly activity) by worldly people because the outer objective world is absent. *Yogins*, on the other hand, call this state *padastham,* which means "being established where you are," because here you become established in your own point. *Yogins* find that *svapna* is a nearer way when entering into *samādhi*, when entering into the absolute. When you are in the state of *jāgrat,* you have to struggle to enter in *samādhi*. When you are in the state of *svapna,* you only have to struggle half as much. It is much easier to concentrate your awareness in *svapna* than it is in *jāgrat*. Children exist primarily in *svapna*. If illuminating

3 sarvatobhadramāsīnaṁ
sarvato vedyasattayā ||
Tantrāloka: X;244

power is put into them by some master or greater soul, they will enter into *samādhi* in an instant. They have no external thoughts; they have only internal thoughts. They are very near to their own Self. *Jñānīs* call the state of *svapna vyāpti*, which means "pervasion," because in the dreaming state they pervade everything and they know that they are pervading. They pervade their own body, the automobile they are dreaming they are driving, the road they are dreaming they are driving on, and the place they are dreaming they are going to. The reality is that none of these objects are produced by any outside agency. All exist within their own self.[4]

Worldly people call the state of deep sleep *suṣupti* (asleep) because they have no knowledge of objectivity in this state. There is no objectivity and there are no impressions. This state is *tūṣṇīmbhāva* which means "absolute silence." For them, it is an appeased state. They feel that after leaving this state they are more peaceful. They find this state to be nourishing. *Yogins*, on the other hand, feel that in this state of sound sleep they become attached to their own nature. This state for *yogins* is full of consciousness, while this state for worldly people is full of unconsciousness. *Yogins*, therefore, call this state *rūpastha*, which means "established in one's own Self," because here they are established in their own Consciousness. *Jñānīs* call this state *mahāvyāpti* (the great pervasion) because here they find that there is absolutely no limitation of objectivity or impressions.

From the Trika Śaivite point of view, predominance is given to the three energies of Śiva, *parā śakti*, the supreme energy; *parāparā śakti*, medium energy; and *aparā śakti*, inferior ener-

---

4 The *jñānī* does not desire to direct his actions in a dream. A *jñānī* is desireless. A *jñānī* does not desire—he just moves. It is Universal Will that acts. The *jñānī* is touched with Universal Will.

gy. The kingdom of *aparā śakti*, the lowest energy, is found in wakefulness and dreaming. The kingdom of *parāparā śakti*, the medium energy, is established in the state of sound sleep. And lastly, the kingdom of *parāśakti*, the supreme energy, is found in the state of *turya*.

The state of *turya* is above the state of *pramātṛi*. It is called the state of *pramiti*. *Pramiti* is that state where subjective consciousness prevails without the agitation of objectivity. Where the agitation of objectivity is also found in subjective consciousness, that is the state of *pramātṛi*. For example, when a person is lecturing and he is full of those objects which he is explaining, this is the state of *pramātṛi*. And when that same experiencer is without the agitation of lectures and there is no objective world before him, this is the state of *pramiti*. The state of *pramiti* is without any object at all. In other words, when he is residing in his own nature, that subjective consciousness is the state of *pramiti*.

The state of *turya* is said to be the penetration of all energies simultaneously, not in succession. All of the energies are residing there but are not in manifestation. They are all together without distinction. *Turya* is called *savyāpārā* because all of the energies get their power to function in that state. At the same time, this state is known as *anāmayā* because it remains unagitated by all of these energies.

Three names are attributed to this state—by worldly people, by *yogins*, and by illuminated humans (*jñānīs*). Worldly people call it *turya*, which means "the fourth." They use this name because they have no descriptive name for this state. They are unaware of this state and, not having experienced it, simply call it the fourth state. *Yogins* have attributed the name *rūpātītā* to this condition because this state has surpassed "the touch of one's self" and is "the establishment of one's self." The touch of one's self was found in sound sleep; however, the establishment of one's self takes place in *turya*. For illuminated humans, *jñānīs*, the entire universal existence is found in this state of *turya*, collectively, as undifferentiated, in the state of totality. There is no succession here. *Jñānīs*, therefore, call this state *pracaya*.[5]

Now I'll explain the names given to the states of *turya jāgrat*, *turya svapna*, and *turya suṣupti*. Only these three states are possible in *turya*. As *turya* cannot be divided, *turya turya* is not possible. The preceding states of individual subjective consciousness, *jāgrat*, *svapna*, and *suṣupti*, each have four aspects; the state of *turya* has only three.

The state of *turya jāgrat* exists when the consciousness of *turya* is not vividly manifested. Here, the consciousness of *turya* is in a subconscious state; it is found in the background. In this state, though strong consciousness exists, it is not manifested totally. It is yet to be manifested. In the state of *turya svapna,* the consciousness of *turya* is more vividly manifested. Consciousness is stronger here. And in the state of *turya suṣupti,* the consciousness of *turya* is the most vivid. Here, consciousness is the strongest. The state of *turya jāgrat* is called *manonmanam,* "beyond the span of the mind," because it is that state where the mind has taken rise in mindlessness, complete thoughtlessness. The state of *turya svapna* is named *anantam,* which means "unlimited" because here is found the unlimited nature of the Self. This is the state of unlimited Being. *Turya suṣupti* is called *sarvārtham. Sarvārtham* means that in this state, although you are unlimited, you find existing all of the limitations of the universe.[6]

---

5 *Pracaya* literally means "totality" and refers to the undifferentiated totality of universal existence.

6 manonmanamanantaṁ ca
sarvārthamiti bhedataḥ
Mālinī Vijaya Tantra: II;46

Turyātīta is that state which is the absolute fullness of Self. It is filled with all consciousness and bliss. It is really the last and the supreme state of the Self. You not only find this state of *turyātīta* in *samādhi*, you also find it in each and every activity of the world. In this state, there is no possibility for the practice of *yoga*. If you can practice *yoga*, then you are not in *turyātīta*. In practicing *yoga*, there is the intention of going somewhere. Here, there is nowhere to go, nothing to achieve. As concentration does not exist here, the existence of the helping hand of *yoga* is not possible.

There are only two names actually attributed to this state of *turyātīta*, one given by worldly people and one by *jñānīs*. Worldly people, because they know nothing about the state, call it *turyātīta*, which means "that state which is beyond the fourth." *Jñānīs*, on the other hand, also have a name for it. They call it *mahāpracaya*,[7] which means "the unlimited and unexplainable supreme totality." *Yogins* do not actually attribute any name to this state because they have no knowledge of it. It is completely outside of their experience. *Yogins* have though, through the use of their imagination and guesswork, imagined one name which might be appropriate for this state: *satatoditam*[8] which means "that state which has no pause, no break." It is a breakless and unitary state. In *samādhi* it is there. When *samādhi* is absent, it is there. In the worldly state it is there. In the dreaming state, it is there. And in the state of deep

---

7 mahāpracayamicchanti
turyātītaṁ vicakṣaṇāḥ ||
Mālinī Vijaya Tantra: II;38

8 turyātīte bheda ekaḥ
satatodita ityayam ||
Tantrāloka: X;283

sleep, it is there. In each and every state of the individual subjective body, it is there.

I have explained the nature of these five states of individual subjectivity from the Trika point of view. In the *Pratyabhijñā* philosophy, the masters of the *Pratyabhijñā* School have also explained and defined these five states. Their definitions of *jāgrat*, *svapna*, and *suṣupti* seem to differ somewhat from that given by the Trika Śaivites. Their explanations of *turya* and *turyātīta*, however, are the same.

The masters of the *Pratyabhijñā* School say that when you remain in that state where your consciousness is directed towards objectivity (*bahirvṛitti*) and you are no longer in your own subjective consciousness, that state is to be known as *jāgrat*. When you remain only in the sphere of impressions and thoughts (*saṁkalpa nirmāṇa*), that state is to be known as *svapna*. And when there is the absolute destruction of all impressions, thoughts, and consciousness (*pralayopamam*), when you are absolutely dead in your own self, that state is to be known as *suṣupti*.

Abhinavagupta, the greatest master of Śaivism and the greatest philosopher the world has ever known, gives the general definition of these states so that the student will know that there is really no difference at all between the Trika Śaivite and the *Pratyabhijñā* points of view. He explains that when there is vividness of objectivity, that is the state of *jāgrat*. When the vividness of objectivity is shaky and unstable, that is *svapna*. When the vividness of objectivity is gone completely that is *suṣupti*. When super-observation is found by some observing agency, that is *turya*. And when that objectivity is individually dead and found full of life in totality, that is *turyātīta*.

Chapter Twelve

The Fivefold Contacts of Masters and Disciples

In this universe from time immemorial the initiation of masters has taken place from Lord Śiva up to the mortal beings. This contact of the master with the disciple takes place in five different ways. The highest contact of the master with the disciple is called *mahān saṁbandhaḥ* (the great contact). This highest contact took place in the very beginning of the manifestation of the universe. Lord Śiva became the master and *Sadāśiva* was the disciple. Next, after this highest contact, a lower contact took place, called *antarāla saṁbandhaḥ*. This is the contact of the master who is residing in the state of *Sadāśiva* with that disciple who is residing in the state of *Anantabhaṭṭāraka*. Then the third contact between master and disciple took place. This third contact is called *divya saṁbandhaḥ,* which means "divine contact." It took place when the master was at the state of *Anantabhaṭṭāraka* and the disciple who was at the state of *Śrīkaṇṭhanātha*. The fourth contact is called *divyādivya saṁbandha*, which means "that contact which is partly divine and partly not divine." In this fourth contact, *Śrīkaṇṭhaḥ* took the place of divinity as the master and *Sanatkumāra Ṛiṣi* took the place of being the disciple. And last, the fifth contact of masters and disciples took place with the masters residing in the place of *Sanatkumāra Ṛiṣi* and the disciples as mortal beings (*manuṣya*). This fifth contact is called *adivya saṁbandha,* which means "that contact which is not divine."

This fifth contact of masters and disciples has occurred many times. In the latest movement of this contact, the master was *Durvāsā Ṛiṣi*, as he was from the school of thought of *Sanatkumāra Ṛiṣi*, and the disciple was *Tryambakanātha*.

Although our Kashmir Śaivism recognizes these fivefold contacts of masters and disciples, yet it explains that only that initiation is a real initiation where the contact of the master and the disciple takes place in such a way that, at the time of initiation, the master is united with the disciple and the disciple is united with the master. In this real initiation the master becomes one with the disciple and the disciple becomes one with the master. You should understand, however, that for this supreme contact to take place, the disciple should never find any fault in his master or his master's activity. If he does, then he is lost. This kind of initiation can take place in any state of these five contacts. It is the real supreme contact. It is even above *mahān saṁbandhaḥ* (the great contact) and is called *para saṁbandhaḥ* (the supreme contact). It is that contact by which all contacts become divine. The real theory of our Śaivism is that this contact, which is the supreme contact, must take place between each and every master and each and every disciple. When this occurs, then that initiation is a real initiation.

Chapter Thirteen

The Birth of the *Tantras*

In the beginning of *satyuga*[1] Lord Śiva appeared in the form of Svacchandanātha. As Svacchandanātha, He appeared with five heads and eighteen arms. His five heads came into manifestation through his five great energies: *cit śakti*, all consciousness; *ānanda śakti*, all bliss; *icchā śakti*, all will; *jñāna śakti*, all knowledge; and *kriyā śakti*, all action. And these five energies, which appeared in His five mouths and which are known as *īśāna, tatpuruṣa, aghora, vāmadeva and sadyojāta*, because of the grace (*anugrahaḥ*)[2] of Lord Śiva, experienced the sensation of illuminating the Universe.

---

1 *Satyuga* is the first age of the four ages *satyuga, tretāyuga, dvāparayuga*, and *kaliyuga*. These comprise the fourfold cyclical life of the universe.

2 The grace (*anugraha*) of Lord Śiva is manifested through His five acts: creation, protection, destruction, concealing, and revealing. In these five acts, Lord Śiva creates the universe, protects it, destroys it, conceals it in His own Nature, and illuminates it. In fact, Lord Śiva creates, protects, destroys, and conceals this universe only to illuminate it.

You see, Lord Śiva wanted to enlighten the universe by manifesting the existence of the *Tantras*. In order to accomplish this, He manifested these *Tantras* through his five mouths. Initially, each of these mouths—*īśāna*, *tatpuruṣa*, *aghora*, *vāmadeva* and *sadyojāta*—created one *Tantra*. Then two mouths joined together and created one *Tantra* from each combination of two mouths. And then three mouths joined together and created one *Tantra* from each combination of three mouths. And then four mouths joined together, and then five mouths, and these combinations of mouths produced all of the *Tantras* of our Śaivism.

These *Tantras* are manifested in three ways. Initially, ten *Tantras* came into existence which were dualistic (*dvaita*) and are called *Śiva Tantras*. These *Tantras*, which are not connected with Kashmir Śaivism, are filled with dualism. Then eighteen *Tantras* came into existence, which were filled with that thought which is monism cum dualism (*bhedābheda*). These *Tantras* are called *Rudra Tantras*. And finally, these five mouths came into existence in such a way that each and every mouth was simultaneously filled with the other four mouths. Here, four of the five energies were inserted into the fifth energy in such a way that it became full with all five energies. No one energy was in predominance, all were equal. And this happened to each and every energy. Simultaneously, from these mouths came the *Bhairava Tantras,* which are filled with only monistic thought (*abheda*). These *Bhairava Tantras*, which are the *Tantras* connected with Kashmir Śaivism, are sixty-four in number.

In the *Bhairava Tantras,* Lord Śiva is shown to be in predominance everywhere. He is there in fullness in Śiva and in all of His energies. He is equally present in everything and everywhere. You cannot say that something is closer to Him and something else is farther away. In everything He is there, fully and completely.

Initially, this monistic *Tantra*, in the form of one Supreme Consciousness and Bliss, was not manifested in will, imagination, or words; rather, it was felt and observed by Lord Śiva Himself at the start of the illuminating energy. At this point, the manifestation of this *Tantra* resided in Lord Śiva's innermost speech, known as *parāvāk* (supreme speech). In this supreme speech of Lord Śiva, the creation of *vācya* and *vācaka*[3], master and disciple, was not yet felt as being differentiated. They resided in His own Being as undifferentiated. In the next movement of illuminating energy, the manifestation of the *Tantras* was held in his second speech, *paśyantī*. At this stage also, these *Tantras* were still undifferentiated and were one with His Supreme Will. In the next movement of illuminating energy, these Tantras were held in His third speech, *madhyamā vāk*. Here, they became differentiated and were manifested internally only in thought not in words. And in the final movement of illuminating energy, these *Tantras* were held in His fourth speech, *vaikharī vāk,* where they came out through His five mouths in differentiation as words, sentences, and verses.

In the three *yugas* (ages), *satyuga*, *tretāyuga*, and *dvāparayuga*, masters and disciples were initiated verbally, not in writing, requiring words and sentences. The power of memory in them was so great that they remembered everything instantaneously. There was no need for them to write anything down or to refer to books and papers. The masters and disciples were very great during these three *yugas.*

When *kaliyuga* occurred, these masters and disciples were so disappointed that they hid themselves in unknown places in order to avoid the touch of worldly people living at that time. Because of this, the theory of the *Bhairava Tantras* and Kashmir Śaivism was lost. Lord Śiva, however, always wishes to illuminate the universe and so He reappeared in this world

3 See pages 12-13 for discussion of *vācya* and *vācaka.*

at Mount Kailāśa, not in the form of Svacchandanātha with five mouths, but in the form of Śrīkaṇṭhanātha. And in the form of Śrīkaṇṭhanātha, He again taught the theory of the *Bhairava Tantras* to the sage Durvāsā Ṛiṣi, who was *ūrdhvaretaḥ*, which means "one whose power of sex is preserved," and who was, therefore, a *brahmacārī* (celibate). When Śrīkaṇṭhanātha initiated him at Mount Kailāśa, Śrīkaṇṭhanātha told him that he was to expand the thought of *Bhairava Tantras* in all of the universe without restriction to caste, color, or creed. After Śrīkaṇṭhanātha taught Durvāsā Ṛiṣi in this manner, he disappeared into the ether.

Durvāsā Ṛiṣi, after meditating completely to acquire a real and fit disciple for initiation, became disappointed. He could not find anyone in this world fit to be initiated. His initiation was a practical initiation because, while initiating someone in the thought of *Bhairava Tantras,* he simultaneously initiated him in the practical side of this thought. And this practical initiation manifested itself immediately without the disciples having to do any practice or *yoga.* This disciple would become instantaneously enlightened. As he could not find a disciple fit for this initiation, he created out of his mental power one mind-born son. This mind-born son was called Tryambakanātha. Durvāsā Ṛiṣi completely initiated Tryambakanātha in the way of the monistic *Bhairava Tantras.* Afterwards, he created two more mind-born sons, Āmardakanātha and Śrīnātha. He initiated his son Āmardakanātha in the dualistic *Śiva Tantras* and he initiated his other son Śrinātha in the monodualistic *Rudra Tantras.* All of this was done by Durvāsā Ṛiṣi for the upliftment of mankind.

For the upliftment of women, Durvāsā Ṛiṣi created one mind-born daughter and she was called Ardhatryambakā.[4] As

4 She was called *Ardhatryambaka* (one-half *Tryambaka*) because, in India and Kashmir, the daughter is considered to be only one-half the property of her father.

Kashmir Śaivism does not recognize women to be in a state of degradation, Durvāsā Ṛiṣi initiated her completely in the monistic thought of *Bhairava Tantras*. As this view, that women are not in a state of degradation, is not held by the other two schools of Śaivism, the dualistic and monodualistic schools, Durvāsā Ṛiṣi created only one-mind born daughter. His daughter Ardhatryambakā's teaching is known as the Ardhatryambaka school of the *Bhairava Tantras*. But as the continuity of the Ardhatryambaka school manifested itself from one woman to another secretly, there is no history of this school in this *kaliyuga*.

Durvāsā Ṛiṣi's son Tryambakanātha, the founder of the monistic school of Śaivism, was also a celibate (*brahmacārī*). According to the way of the sage Durvāsā Ṛiṣi, he also created one mind-born son and named him Tryambakāditya, which means "the expansion of Tryambakanātha." After initiating him completely in *Bhairava Tantras*, Tryambakanātha entered a cave, which is known as Tryambaka Guhā (cave), and disappeared. Tryambakanātha's son Tryambakāditya also created one mind-born son and, after initiating him, Tryambakāditya disappeared into the ether.[4]

In this manner fifteen *siddhas* were created by mind. When, however, the fifteenth *siddha* attempted to create a mind-born son, he was not successful. It is said that this fifteenth *siddha* was not fully introverted, but at the same time he was also given to worldly pleasures. Because of this subtle impurity (*āṇava mala*), he was not successful in creating a mind-born son. After sitting in long meditation, he found in this world a girl with all good qualities and he went to her father and made arrangements to marry her. After marriage, they created one son who was called Saṁgamāditya and who, by his will, came

5 These sages were not born through sex; they were "mind-born." As they were *siddhas*, which are spiritual beings without any experience of physical limitations, they did not die; they simply disappeared.

to the valley of Kashmir and found Kailāśa mountain. Saṁgamāditya, like his father, married and produced one son named Varṣāditya, whom he initiated completely in the thought of the monistic *Bhairava Tantras*. Varṣāditya also married and produced one son, named Aruṇāditya, whom he initiated fully. Aruṇāditya married and created one son named Ānanda, whom he initiated and who was also completely informed practically in Śaivism.

This sage Ānanda was the father of Somānandanātha, the originator of the Pratyabhijñā School of Śaivism and the author of the "*Śiva Dṛiṣṭi.*" Up to the time of Somānandanātha, the initiation into the monistic thought of *Bhairava Tantras* took place from father to son. From Somānandanātha on, this initiation took place from master to disciple. Somānandanātha was the master of Utpaladeva. Utpaladeva was the master of Lakṣmaṇagupta. And Lakṣmaṇagupta was a master of our great Abhinavagupta, who was in the line of Atrigupta.

Now I will explain to you how this Atrigupta, a great scholar of Kashmir Śaivism, came from India to live in the Kashmir Valley.

During his reign, the king Lalitāditya traveled to India from Kashmir, where in Antarvedi, a tract of land in Madhya Pradesh which lies between the Yamuna and Ganges rivers, he discovered this great Śaiva teacher Atrigupta. Lalitāditya was deeply impressed by the scholarship and practical way of Atrigupta and requested him to accompany him to the Kashmir Valley. Atrigupta agreed and upon reaching Kashmir, was given the old palace of Pravarasena to live in because it was very near to the palace of the king Lalitāditya. After he moved to Kashmir, there was no authority on Kashmir Śaivism left in India. From this time forward, the teaching of the thought of Bhairava Tantras is called Kashmir Śaivism and this teaching has continued to remain centered only in the Kashmir Valley. These *Bhairava Tantras* are pervasive throughout the whole world. However, they began in the Kashmir Valley, resided there, and are still alive there today. After some centuries in the house of Atrigupta, Varāhagupta was born. He is the father of Narasiṁhagupta and Narasiṁhagupta is the father of our great Abhinavagupta. Although Abhinavagupta had many disciples, both men and women, his chief disciple was Kṣemarāja and the chief disciple of Kṣemarāja was Yogarāja. After many centuries in the Kashmir Valley, Svāmī Ram came into this physical body. His chief disciple was Svāmī Mahatābakak and I am the disciple of Svāmī Mahatābakak.

Chapter Fourteen

Mokṣa in Kashmir Śaivism and Indian Philosophy

The view that ignorance is the cause of bondage and perfect knowledge is the cause of freedom (*mokṣa*) is commonly accepted by all Indian philosophers. Yet, in reality, these philosophers have not completely understood knowledge and ignorance.

The *Vaiṣṇavites*, for example, believe that liberation (*mokṣa*) from repeated births and deaths occurs when you are united with *parāprakṛiti*.[1] And this union with *parāprakṛiti*

---

1 *Prakṛiti* is explained in the *śāstras* (scriptures) in two ways. *Aparā prakṛiti*, which is said to be eightfold, is the combination of the five great elements, along with mind, intellect, and ego.

pañcemāni mahābāho
kāraṇāni nibodha me ǀ
sāṁkhye kṛitānte proktāni
siddhaye sarvakarmaṇām ǁ

Bhagavadgītā XVIII:13

Parāprakṛiti is that energy of being which governs and contains all the activities and conceptions of this universe.

will take place only when you observe in your understanding that the apparent differentiation of this universe is unreal. Then all attachments, pleasures, and pains will come to an end and you will be established in your own real nature. It is this establishment which, from their point of view, is called *mokṣa*.

The *Advaita Vedāntins*, on the other hand, have concluded that, in the real sense, *mokṣa* is only bliss (*ānanda*) and nothing else. They say that when you are residing in the field of ignorance (*saṁsāra*), you become the victim of the fivefold veils: *avidyā* (ignorance), *asmitā* (ego), *rāga* (attachment), *dveṣa* (hatred) and *abhiniveṣa* (attachment to your own conception). These coverings, which are the cause of your remaining in *saṁsāra*, should be removed by the practice of *tattvajñāna*. In this practice, you must mentally negate all that is not your own real nature by thinking, *neti*, *neti*, "I am not this, I am not this." So here you practice thinking, "I am not the physical body, I am not the subtle body, I am not the mind, I am not the life essence (*prāṇa*)." You must negate all outside elements. And when you reside completely in your own nature, which is that which remains after you negate all outside elements, that knowledge, from their point of view, is called *mokṣa*.

The tradition of *Buddhist* philosophers, who are known as the *Vijñānavādins*, accept, that you are liberated only when your mind is completely detached from all attachments to objectivity, pleasure, pain, and sorrow. They argue that the mind must remain only as mind, pure and perfect mind, because for them the mind is actually pure, filled with light, and detached from all worldly things. It is when the mind becomes attached to worldly things, such as thoughts, pleasures, and pains, that you are carried to *saṁsāra*. And when these attachments are cancelled and the mind becomes pure, then you are liberated.

The philosophers from the *Vaibhāṣika* tradition hold that liberation is attained by eliminating the chain of thoughts, just as the flame of a lamp is extinguished. When a lamp is burning, we experience the existence of the flame. When, however, the flame is extinguished, it does not go anywhere. It does not go into the earth or into the ether. When the flame is extinguished, it simply disappears. And the extinguishing of the flame takes place when the oil of the lamp is exhausted. In the same way, when a *yogī* has crossed over all the pleasures and pains of the world, those pleasures and pains do not go anywhere, they simply disappear. This *yogī*, who has extinguished the flame of the chain of thoughts by exhausting the wax of the five *kleśas,*[2] enters into the supreme and perfect peace which is, from their point of view, liberation.

From the Śaivite point of view, these philosophical traditions remain either in *apavedyapralayākala* or in *savedyapralayākala*. They do not go beyond these states. *Apavedyapralayākala* is that state of *pralayākala* where there is no objectivity. *Savedyapralayākala* is that state of *pralayākala* where there is some impression of objectivity. As an example, take the state of deep sleep. When you wake up from deep sleep and then think, "I was sleeping and I didn't know anything," that is the state of *apavedyapralayākala*. And when you wake up from the state of deep sleep and think, "I was sleeping peacefully without dreaming," that is the state of *savedyapralayākala* because you experienced that it was a sweet sleep and so "sweetness" is the object for you in this state. Śaiva philosophy does not recognize the theories of

2 *Kleśas*, which means, literally, "pains, misfortune," are afflictions which delude you and lead you astray. In *Yoga* philosophy these afflictions are fivefold: *avidyā* (ignorance), *asmitā* (ego), *rāga* (attachment), *dveṣa* (hatred), and *abhiniveṣa* (attachment to your own conception).

these philosophies concerning *mokṣa* because, in fact, the *yogins* of these traditions do not move above the *pralayākala* state and are not, therefore, situated in real *mokṣa*.

Our Śaivism explains that *jñāna* (knowledge) is knowing one's own nature, which is all Being (*sat*), all consciousness (*cit*), and all bliss (*ānanda*). *Ajñāna* (ignorance) is ignoring this nature and this is the cause of the *saṁsāra* which carries one in the cycle of repeated births and deaths.

Kashmir Śaivism explains that ignorance (*ajñāna*) is of two kinds: *pauruṣa ajñāna* and *bauddha ajñāna*. *Pauruṣa ajñāna* is that kind of ignorance wherein one is unaware of realizing one's own nature in *samādhi*. This kind of ignorance is removed by the grace of masters and by meditating upon one's own Self. And when this ignorance is removed, you find yourself in the real knowledge of Śaivism, which is all being, all consciousness, all bliss. This kind of knowledge is called *pauruṣa jñāna*. When you possess *pauruṣa jñāna,* you realize your nature of Self perfectly.

Bauddha ajñāna (intellectual ignorance) occurs only when you are completely ignorant of the philosophical truth of the monistic idea of Śaivism. And *bauddha ajñāna* is removed by studying those monistic Śaiva texts which explain the reality of the Self. Therefore, these texts are the cause of your being carried from *bauddha ajñāna* to *bauddha jñāna*. *Bauddha jñāna* is thought-based and is developed through the intellect. *Pauruṣa jñāna*, on the other hand, is practical and is developed through practice. *Pauruṣa jñāna* is predominant over *bauddha jñāna* because when you possess only *pauruṣa jñāna,* even then you are liberated in the real sense. In this case, however, liberation is attained only after leaving your body. When, however, at the same time, you attach *bauddha jñāna* to *pauruṣa jñāna*, which means that, on the one hand, you practice on your own Being and, on the other hand, you go into the philosophical thought of the monistic Śaiva texts and elevate your intellectual being, then you become a *jīvanmukta*, one who is liberated while living. If, however, you possess only *bauddha jñāna* and not *pauruṣa jñāna,* then you will not attain liberation either while living in the body or at the time of death. *Bauddha jñāna* without *pauruṣa jñāna* is useless and will not take you anywhere. The study of texts shines perfectly only when there is practical knowledge at the same time. Without practical knowledge, philosophical study is useless. *Bauddha jñāna* will bear fruit only when *pauruṣa jñāna* is present and not otherwise.

If an aspirant is attached only to practical knowledge and not to theoretical knowledge, believing that the only real knowledge is practical knowledge, which is the realizing of ones own nature, then from a Śaiva point of view he is mistaken. If only *pauruṣa jñāna* is cultivated and *bauddha jñāna* is totally ignored, then there is every possibility that *pauruṣa jñāna* may decrease day by day, slowly fading away so that in the end, it does not remain at all. It is the greatness of *bauddha jñāna* that, with its power, it firmly establishes *pauruṣa jñāna.* In this respect, therefore, *bauddha jñāna* is more important than *pauruṣa jñāna.*

In our Śaivism, it is said that when you go in search of a master so that you can be initiated, you should first seek that master who is full of both *bauddha jñāna* and *pauruṣa jñāna.* Finding him, you should consider him a real master. If in this world such a complete master is not to be found, then you should seek one who is only filled with *bauddha jñāna.* He is to be preferred over that master who is filled only with *pauruṣa jñāna* because intellectually he will carry you by and by to the end point. That master who resides only in *pauruṣa jñāna* would not ultimately be successful in carrying you to that which you seek.

Chapter Fifteen

Kashmir Śaivism and Advaita Vedānta

Although the main principle of both Kashmir Śaivism and *Vedānta* is monism (*advaita*), pure monism, yet there are many important differences in their thinking. For example, *Vedānta* masters teach that *karmayoga* means *yoga* in action. They believe that you must practice *niḥṣkāma karmayoga,* which means that you are to perform all the actions of the world without asking for any reward. They say that by acting in this way you are carried toward the existence of the Real Being, the Real Nature of Self. From our Kashmir Śaiva point of view, however, *karmayoga* means something else. It does not mean carrying out all of the activities of the world. *Yoga* in action is pure *yoga* and nothing else. *Pure* yoga is one-pointedness, and this one-pointedness must be developed in three ways. You must develop one-pointedness in the existence of your being. This is one-pointedness in the state of *parā vāk* (supreme speech). You must also develop one-pointedness in the state of *madhyamā vāk* (medium speech). And finally, you must develop one-pointedness in the state of *vaikharī vāk* (inferior speech), in the state of ordinary speech.

In Śaivism, we begin with the central way, the way of *madhyamā vāk.* Kashmir Śaivism explains that *yoga* in action means that when you are seated in a bus, or when you are walking on the road, you must observe silence. Walk silently, sit in the bus silently. Do not talk to anybody. Continue your practice of contemplating Lord Śiva as you were instructed by your Master, without talking to anybody. This is how you begin. It is not possible at first to practice *yoga* while talking. In the beginning, you have to start with silence.

This *yoga* in action is tremendously powerful. For example, if you were to continue your practice of contemplation for just fifteen minutes while walking, the benefit will be the same as you would acquire if you were to continuously practice contemplation in your meditation room for two or even three years. This is because *yoga* in action makes your practice of contemplation more firm, solid, and substantial. This is why Kashmir Śaivism puts stress on *yoga* in action, and not on that *yoga* which is inactive.

In the practice of *yoga* in action in *madhyamā vāk,* you begin with silence. And when you rise from *madhyamā,* you will rise in the *parā* state of Śiva. This *parā* state will occur, however, only when you have completed your activity. For example, while practicing your contemplation, you take a ten mile walk, five miles going and five miles returning, after which you go home, where you sit in meditation. At this point, you will automatically enter the *parā* state of *yoga* in action and this will carry you rapidly to that state of Transcendental Being. You must enter into the *parā* state of *yoga* in action automatically. You cannot make it happen. If it does not happen, then you will have to begin again practicing contemplation in action. It is by the strength of *yoga* in action that you enter into the *parā* state of *yoga.* If your contemplation in action is spontaneous and breakless, then you will automatically enter into the *parā* state of *yoga.* If, on the other hand, your contemplation breaks at any time while practicing, then when you sit for meditation, contemplation on *parā* will not take place and you will have to begin again. This is called *karmayoga.*

When you are established in the *yoga* of action in *parā vāk,* then, after some time, you have to travel from *parā vāk* to *vaikharī vāk.* Practicing *yoga* in action in *vaikharī vāk* means that you are to remain established in your own being while talking, while laughing, while carrying out all of the actions of the world. This kind of yoga in action in *vaikharī vāk* is not possible unless *yoga* in action in *madhyamā vāk* and *yoga* in action in *parā vāk* are complete. The sign of their being complete is that whenever you practice *yoga* in action in *madhyamā vāk* and afterwards you sit and meditate, you enter into *parā vāk,* you are inside, residing in your own Nature. Establishing *yoga* in action in *vaikharī vāk* is the completion of the course of *yoga* in action. Here, you remain established in your own Being in all the activities of the world. It is said that Lord Kṛiṣṇa was perfectly established in *yoga* in action in *vaikharī.* He was very active, doing everything while remaining established in his own nature.

The first difference, therefore, between Kashmir Śaivism and *Vedānta* is in their different understanding of *karmayoga.* This difference, as you have seen, is very great, with the *Vedāntins* believing that *karmayoga* means doing all actions without asking for their reward and our Kashmir Śaivism teaching that *yoga* in action means doing all actions while maintaining a breakless contemplation of God.

Another difference between Kashmir Śaivism and *Vedānta* concerns the existence of individual being and Universal Being. The *Vedāntins* explain that individual being is manifested only when Universal Being is reflected in the mirror of the individual intellect. They say that Universal Being is reflected in the intellect (*buddhi*) and that reflection becomes the existence of the individual being (*jīva*). Kashmir Śaivism, however, does not recognize this explanation, arguing that it is without any basis. As Universal Being is absolutely pure and perfect and individual being is filled with imperfections (*malas*) and covered by veils, it is not *buddhi* that will reflect Universal Being, but rather, it is Universal Being that will reflect *buddhi*. It is the purer and more refined reality which will take the reflection of that which is less pure and refined and not the other way around. *Buddhi* cannot hold Universal Being. Kashmir Śaivism explains that when Śiva is reflected by His pure will in the mirror of his freedom (*svātantrya*), this is the existence of the universe and the existence of individual being.

Furthermore, in the theory of the *Vedāntins,* it is not clearly explained how, if the world were not existing, *buddhi*, in which Lord Śiva is to be reflected, could exist at all. How could the intellect (*buddhi*) exist before the existence of the world? Therefore, individual being is the reflection of Lord Śiva in His *svātantrya śakti*. This is the existence of the universe.

The third area of difference between Kashmir Śaivism and *Vedānta* concerns the essence, the substance, the basis of this universe. *Vedānta* holds that this universe is untrue, unreal. It does not really exist. It is only the creation of illusion (*māyā*). Concerning this point, Kashmir Śaivism argues that if Lord Śiva is real, then how could an unreal substance come out from something that is real? If Lord Śiva is real, then His creation is also real. Why should it be said that Lord Śiva is real and His creation is an illusion (*māyā*)? Kashmir Śaivism explains that the existence of this universe is just as real as the existence of Lord Śiva. As such, it is true, real, pure, and solid. There is nothing at all about it which is unreal.

The fourth important difference between Kashmir Śaivism and *Vedānta* is that *Vedānta* does not recognize *kuṇḍalinī yoga*. The *Vedāntins* say that *kuṇḍalinī yoga* is meant for those who are treading on the inferior path of *yoga*. From our Kashmir Śaivite point of view, however, *kuṇḍalinī yoga* is the most important *yoga* in this system. Kashmir Śaivism explains that there are three paths of *kuṇḍalinī yoga*: *parā kuṇḍalinī yoga*, *cit kuṇḍalinī yoga*, and *prāṇa kuṇḍalinī yoga*. *Parā kuṇḍalinī yoga* is supreme *kuṇḍalinī yoga*. It is functioned by Lord Śiva with the universal body, not the individual body. *Cit kuṇḍalinī yoga* is *kuṇḍalinī* in consciousness. *Prāṇa kuṇḍalinī yoga* is *kuṇḍalinī* in breath.

The fifth significant difference between Kashmir Śaivism and *Vedānta* concerns the question of who is fit to practice this monistic teaching. *Vedānta* holds that this teaching can only be practiced by "worthy people" such as *brahmins* with "good qualities." In fact, Śaṁkarācārya holds that *Vedānta* is meant only for *saṁyāsins*[1] and not others. From the *Vedāntic* point of view, women and other castes are not allowed to practice the *Vedāntic* system. This point of view, however, is not recognized by our Kashmir Śaivism. Kashmir Śaivism teaches that this monistic thought can be practiced by anyone, man or woman, without the restriction of caste, creed, or color. In fact, our Śaivism teaches us that this thought can be practiced more fruitfully by women than by men.[2]

1 *Saṁyāsins* are "ascetics," those who have renounced all earthly concerns and have devoted themselves to meditation and the study of the *Āraṇyakas* and *Upaniṣads*, etc.

2. yoktā saṁvatsarātsiddhir
iha puṁsāṁ bhayātmanam |
sā siddhistattvaniṣṭhānāṁ
strīṇāṁ dvādaśabhirdinaiḥ ||

"That attainment which is said to be achieved in one year's time by those terrified is achieved in twelve days by those divine ladies who are established in the true path of Śaivism."

Quoted by Jayaratha in his commentary of Tantrāloka I:13

Kashmir Śaivism, therefore, is a universal system, pure, real, and substantial in every respect, which can be practiced by all.

Chapter Sixteen

The Seven States of *Turya*

The practical theory of the seven states of *turya,* also known as the seven states of *ānanda* (bliss), which I will now explain to you, was taught to the great Śaivite philosopher Abhinavagupta by his master Śaṁbhunātha.

Between the three states of the individual subjective body, waking, dreaming, and deep sleep, there is a gap. This gap is a junction between the waking state and the dreaming state. There is also a junction between the dreaming state and dreamless sound sleep and there is a junction between sound sleep and the waking state. These transitions take place automatically within every human being. Whenever you pass from wakefulness to the dreaming state, you touch that junction and then enter into the dreaming state. Whenever you pass from the dreaming state to wakefulness, you touch that junction first and then you open your eyes and experience the waking state. This junction is touched whenever you pass between any of the three states of the individual subjective body. This junction is actually the fourth state, *turya*. This *turya*, however, cannot be experienced by focusing on it because, whenever you gaze on this junction, waiting for it to happen, it will never happen. You will remain waiting in the waking state. It is when you fall asleep and enter into the dreaming state that you will find it. And yet ordinarily you remain absolutely unaware of the experience of this junction.

The only way to experience this junction is to concentrate on any center of the heart while breathing, while talking, or while moving about. You must concentrate on the center. You should watch the center of any two movements, any two breaths. Concentrate on that junction. After some time when that concentration is established, then whenever you go to bed to rest, you will automatically enter the dreaming state through that junction. In this case though, you will not enter into the dreaming state. Instead, you will be aware at that point, at that junction. This junction is only a gate, the entrance to *turya*. Your awareness of this junction occurs only by the grace of your previous practice of centering your mind between any two movements or any two breaths. This is the first state of *turya*, called *nijānanda*[1] which means "the bliss of your own Self."

You first experience that junction while practicing on any center, such as that found between any two breaths, between any two movements, or between any two thoughts. When you concentrate in continuity with great reverence, with love, affection, and devotion, then your breath becomes very fine and subtle. Automatically, you breathe very slowly. At that moment, you experience giddiness. It is a kind of intoxicating mood. And when, during the experience of this giddiness, you do not destroy your alertness of concentration, the giddiness becomes firm and stable. This is the second state of *turya*,

1. nijānande pramātraṁśamātre hṛidi purā sthitaḥ
Tantrāloka: V;44

known as *nirānanda*[2] which means "devoid of limited bliss." Here you do not lose awareness, even though you feel intoxicated. And when that giddiness becomes stable and remains for a longer period, then the aspirant falls asleep at once. Yet at this point he does not enter into the dreaming state; rather, he enters that gap, that junction. This junction is known to be the start of *turya*. In entering this junction, the aspirant enters into another world. It is not wakefulness, nor is it the dreaming state, nor is it sound sleep, but a fourth world. Here, the organs of this aspirant do not function at all. He does not experience moving about nor does he hear or see. If, with great effort, he were to open his eyes, he would feel that he is still sitting in his house; however, actually he cannot move any part of his body and can only slightly move his eyelids.

At that moment, the aspirant hears hideous sounds and sees furious forms. Those aspirants who are frightened by these things try at once to come out from this state and, after exerting great effort, they come out and are again in the waking state. On the other hand, there are those aspirants who try to tolerate these hideous and terrible things. For example, he may experience that the whole of the house has collapsed upon him or he may experience that there is a fire burning outside and this fire will burn everything including himself. These experiences, if endured and tolerated, will pass away. If the aspirant cannot tolerate them, then he will be thrown out into the waking state and must begin again. The aspirant, in order to continue his journey, must tolerate these hideous and terrible experiences. Here, only one thing is predominant and must be maintained and that is breathing. The aspirant must breathe in and out with devotion and great love towards his Self. This means

2 śūnyatāmātraviśranternirānandaṁ vibhāvayet
Tantrāloka: V;44

to breathe in and out while reciting the name of the Lord, as he was instructed by his master when he was initiated, all the while ignoring these terrible sounds. He may actually think that he is going to die, that he is really gone. These thoughts are wrong thoughts and he must ignore them. When the aspirant desires to move from individuality to universality, all of these experiences occur because individuality has to be shaken off. When this movement toward universality begins, this kind of struggle takes place.

If you continue with tolerance, breathing and internally reciting your *mantra* according to the instructions of your master, then these terrible sounds and forms vanish and pulling and pushing in your breathing passage begins to occur. You feel as if you are choking and that you cannot breathe. This experience you must also undergo and tolerate. You must insert more love and affection for your practice because the more devotion you have the more chocking you will experience. If this is done, then after some time, this choking sensation will pass. If, however, at this point you do not intensify the devotion for your practice, then you will come out from this state and will need to begin again afresh. If this occurs, you will feel foolish and realize that by not tolerating these experiences, you have caused a great loss to yourself. Because of this, you will be anxious to begin again.

This state of hideous sounds and forms, followed by the sensation that you are choking and that your breathing is about to stop, is called *parānanda,*[3] which means "the *ānanda* (bliss) of breathing." When you breathe in and out with great divinity, it is not ordinary breathing. Here, your breathing becomes full of bliss and joy, even though you are experiencing terrible forms

3 prāṇodaye prameye tu parānandaṁ vibhavayet
Tantrāloka: V;45

and sounds or the reality that your breath is about to stop.

If you maintain your practice continuously with intense devotion, your breath does stop. What happens is that four passages meet at the center of what we call *lambikā sthāna* which in English is known as the "soft palate." This *lambikā sthāna* is found on the right side near the pit of the throat. In ordinary breathing, two passages are open and two passages are closed. When your breath is about to stop, the passages of ordinary breathing close. You experience this symptom when you feel that you are choking and that your breath is about to stop. At this point, your breath becomes centralized and moves about one point, just like a whirlpool. The aspirant experiences that his breath is neither moving out nor coming in. He feels that his breath is moving round and round, that it is rotating at that one point which is the junction of the four passages. This state is called *bhramānanda,*[4] which means, "that bliss which is all-pervading."

Here, the *yogin* must maintain the continuity of his devotional practice. As his breathing has stopped and he cannot watch his breath, he can only recite *mantras*. He must put his mind on his *mantra,* and only his *mantra,* with great devotion to Lord Śiva. If he continues this practice with great devotion, then, after some time, yawning takes place or his mouth becomes crooked, just as it happens at the moment of death. These stages are the same stages which take place when your breath has stopped and you are about to die. The myriad of changes that take place on his face are those that take place at the moment of death. The apprehension of death then arises in

4 samānabhūmimāgatya brahmānandamayo bhavet
Tantrāloka: V;47

"The equilibrium of breath, neither breathing in nor breathing out is *brahmānanda*."

the mind of this *yogī*. He feels now that he is really dying. He is not afraid, he is apprehensive. This is the kind of death which takes place when individuality dies and universality is born. It is not a physical death; it is a mental death. The only thing the *yogī* must do here is to shed tears of devotion. He must pray for the experience of universal "I." After a few moments, when the whirling state of breath becomes very fast, moving ever more quickly, you must stop your breath at once. You must not be afraid. If your master is there, he will tell you at that moment to just stop your breath. When there is the whirling of breath, then there is the possibility that you may start breathing again. At this point, it is in your hand to stop it or to let it go. When it has come to the extreme intensity of whirling, then you should and must stop it at once!

When you stop your breathing, then what happens next is that your breath immediately rushes down in the central vein. Your breath is "sipped" down and you actually hear the sound of sipping. The gate of the central vein (*madhyanāḍī*) opens at once and your breath reaches down to that place called *mūlādhāra,* which is near the rectum. This state of *turya* is called *mahānanda*[5] which means, "the great bliss."

After *mahānanda,* no effort is required by the aspirant. From this point on, everything is automatic. There is, however, one thing that the aspirant should observe and be cautious about and that is that he should not think that "everything is now automatic." The more he thinks that everything will be automatic, the more surely he will remain at the state of *mahānanda*. This is why masters never tell the aspirant what will take

5. udānavahnau viśrānto mahānandaṁ vibhāvayan
Tantrāloka: V;48

place after *mahānanda*.

From the Śaiva point of view, from *mahānanda* onwards, you must adopt *bhramavega*.[6] *Bhramavega* means "the unknowing force." Here you have to put your force of devotion, without knowing what is to happen next. You cannot use your *mantra* because when your breath is gone, your mind is also gone, as the mind has become transformed into the formation of consciousness (*cit*). Here, breathing takes the form of force (*vega*). It is this *vega* which pierces and penetrates *mūlādhāra cakra* so that you pass through it.

When the penetration of *mūlādhāra cakra* is complete, then this force rises in another way. It is transformed and becomes full of bliss, full of ecstasy, and full of consciousness. It is divine. You feel what you are actually. This is the rising of *cit kuṇḍalinī,* which rises from *mūlādhāra cakra* to that place at the top of the skull known as *brahmarandhra*. It occupies the whole channel and is just like the blooming of a flower. This state, which is the sixth state of *turya*, is called *cidānanda*,[7] which means, "the bliss of consciousness."

This force then presses the passage of the skull (*brahmarandhra*), piercing the skull to move from the body out into the universe. This takes place automatically; it is not to be "done." And when this *brahmarandhra* is pierced, then at once you begin to breathe out. You breathe out once for only a second, exhaling from the nostrils. After exhaling, everything is over and you are again in *cidānanda* and you again experience

6 tāvadvai bhramavegena mathanaṁ śaktivigrahe |
vedattu prathamotpannā viṅdavaste'tivarcasaḥ ||
Tantrasadbhāva,
quoted in Śiva Sūtra Vimarśinī II:3

7 nirupādhirmahāvyāptirvyānākhyopādhivarjitā |
tadā khalu cidānando yo jaḍānupabṛiṁhitaḥ ||
Tantrāloka: V;49

and feel the joy of rising, which was already present. This lasts only for a moment and then you breathe out again. When you breathe out, your eyes are open and for a moment you feel that you are outside. You experience the objective world, but in a peculiar way. Then once again, your breathing is finished and your eyes are closed and you feel that you are inside. Then again your eyes are open for a moment, then they close for a moment, and then they again open for a moment. This is the state of *krama mudrā*, where transcendental "I" consciousness is beginning to be experienced as one with the experience of the objective world.

The establishment of *krama mudrā* is called *jagadānanda,*[8] which means "universal bliss." This is the seventh and last state of *turya*. In this state, the experience of Universal Transcendental Being is never lost and the whole of the universe is experienced as one with your own Transcendental "I" Consciousness.

All of the states of *turya* from *nijānanda* to *cidānanda* comprise the various phases of *nimīlanā samādhi*. *Nimīlanā samādhi* is internal subjective *samādhi*. In your moving through these six states of *turya,* this *samādhi* becomes ever more firm. With the occurrence of *krama mudrā*, *nimīlanā samādhi* is transformed into *unmīlanā samādhi,* which then becomes predominant. This is that state of extroverted *samādhi,* where you experience the state of *samādhi* at the same time you are experiencing the objective world. And when *unmīlanā samādhi* becomes fixed and permanent, this is the state of *jagadānanda*.

---

8 yatra ko'pi vyavacchedo nasti yadviśvataḥ sphurat ||
yadanāhata-saṁvitti paramāmṛita bṛiṁhitam |
yatrāsti bhāvanādīnāṁ na mukhyā kāpi saṁgatiḥ ||
tadeva jagadānanda ......|

Tantrāloka: V;50-52

In terms of the process of the fifteen-fold rising, the *sakala* state is the waking state. *Sakala pramātṛi* is the first state of *turya,* which is the state of *nijānanda*. *Vijñānākala*[9] is the state of *nirānanda*. *Śuddhavidyā* is the state of *parānanda*. *Īśvara* is the state of *brahmānanda*. *Sadāśiva* is the state of *mahānanda*. Śiva is the state of *cidānanda*. And Parama Śiva is the state of *jagadānanda*.

There is a point twixt sleep and waking
Where thou shalt be alert without shaking.
Enter into the new world where forms so hideous pass;
They are passing—endure, do not be taken by the dross.
Then the pulls and the pushes about the throttle,
All those shalt thou tolerate.
Close all ingress and egress,
Yawnings there may be;
Shed tears—crave—implore, but thou will not prostrate.
A thrill passes—and that goes down to the bottom;
It riseth, may it bloom forth, that is Bliss.
Blessed Being! Blessed Being!
O greetings be to Thee!

Swami Lakshmanjoo Brahmachari

---

9 From the state of *vijñānākala,* the process of rising is automatic. Though there may be something to be done, this something is neither physical nor mental. Once the aspirant has attained the *vijñānākala* state, he will never fall. If, for example, the aspirant once enters the state of *vijñānākala* between waking and sleeping, then during his lifetime he will never lose that state. Whenever he does his practice in continuity with devotion, he will enter the *vijñānākala* state. This is because once the *vijñānākala* state has been experienced, it leaves a permanent impression. At this point, you

are not in the state of *pramātṛi;* you are in the state of *vijñānākala. Vijñānākala pramātṛi* is much higher than the state of *vijñānākala. Vijñānākala pramātṛi* takes place after *śuddhavidyā*. The difference between *vijñānākala pramātṛi* and the state of *vijñānākala* is that the state of *vijñānākala* is ordinary, while *vijñānākala pramātṛi* is special and more significant. This is also the case with all of the states and their *pramātṛins.* When you unknowingly experience a state, then you are in that which is called a "state." When you knowingly experience any state, which means that you are active in that process, that is the state of *pramātṛi.* For example, when you enter in *samādhi,* you are not in the *pramātṛi* state of *samādhi*, rather you are simply in the state of *samādhi.* At this point, you have no control over this state. You will enter into this state according to the choice of your master or Lord Śiva. Sometimes you will wish to enter this state and you do enter it, and sometimes you will wish to enter this state and yet you cannot enter it. You can be said to be in the state of *pramātṛi* only when you have the full authority of going to that state and returning from it whenever you wish to do so.

Chapter Seventeen

***Kuṇḍalinī* and Its Purpose**

Kuṇḍalinī śakti is the revealing and the concealing energy of Lord Śiva. On the one hand, it is the revealing energy and on the other hand, it is the concealing energy. It reveals and it conceals. This *kuṇḍalinī śakti* is not different from the existence of Lord Śiva, just as the energy of light and the energy of heat are not separate from the fire itself. *Kuṇḍalinī*, therefore, in the true sense, is the existence of Śiva. It is the life and glory of Śiva. It is Śiva Himself.

In our Trika Śaivism, *kuṇḍalinī*, which is that internal serpent power existing in the shape of a coil, is divided in three ways. The supreme *kuṇḍalinī* is called *parā kuṇḍalinī*. This *kuṇḍalinī* is not known or experienced by *yogins*. It is so vast and universal that the body cannot exist in its presence. It is only experienced at the time of death. It is the heart of Śiva. This whole universe is created by *parā kuṇḍalinī*, exists in *parā kuṇḍalinī*, gets its life from *parā kuṇḍalinī*, and is consumed in *parā kuṇḍalinī*. When this *kuṇḍalinī* creates the universe, Śiva conceals His Real Nature and is thrown into the universe. When the universe is created, He becomes the universe. There is no Śiva left which is separate from the universe. This is His creative energy. And when *kuṇḍalinī* destroys the universe, Śiva's nature is revealed. So, the creative energy for the universe is the destructive energy for Śiva, i.e., it is the revealing energy for the universe and the concealing energy for Lord Śiva. And the destructive energy for the universe is the creative energy for Śiva, i.e., it is the concealing energy for the universe and the revealing energy for Lord Śiva.[1]

Parā kuṇḍalinī is the supreme *visarga* of Śiva. As you know from studying the theory of *mātṛikācakra*, *visarga* [:] comprises two points. These points are said to be Śiva and Śakti. In the real sense, however, these points are not Śiva and Śakti; they are the revealing point and the concealing point.

Cit kuṇḍalinī is experienced by *yogins* by means of concentrating on the center between any two breaths, thoughts, or actions, between the destruction and creation of any two things. As you have learned in your study of the seven states of *turya*, when the *yogin* maintains his awareness continually in concentrating on the center, he enters that junction which exists between any two states of the individual subjective body, waking, dreaming, or deep sleep. His breathing becomes coagulated, then stops and whirls about one point. It then moves on the right side of the passage of the breath. If this *yogin's* awareness continues to be maintained with continuity, his breath is transformed from *prāṇa* (breath) into *prāṇana* (life) and it rushes down through the central vein, which is on the right side[2] of the

---

1 When Lord Śiva is concealed, He is in the state of *Anuttara Śiva*. When He is revealed, He is then said to be in the state of *Maheśvara Śiva*.

2 There is only one vein through which the breath passes in the rise of *kuṇḍalinī*. When the breath is being sipped down, it is sipped down on the right side and when it is returning, it is in the center. The conception of *iḍā*, *piṅgalā*, and *suṣumnā* is a gross conception. It is only descriptive of

passage of the breath. It rushes down to the bottom, to the spot known as *mūlādhāra*, which is near the rectum. Then in *mūlādhāra,* you briefly experience a crawling sensation. It is like the experience when a man and a woman are having intercourse and sexual climax is just about to take place. Here, the beginning of intense pleasure occurs. After the momentary experience of this crawling sensation, it rises again in one flash.[3] And when it rises, you become filled with absolutely blissful existence. The happiness and bliss that you experience here cannot be described. It is ecstasy beyond ecstasy, just like sexual bliss. In comparing sexual happiness with the happiness experienced in *cit kuṇḍalinī*, however, you will find that sexual happiness is one millionth part of the happiness experienced in *cit kuṇḍalinī.* In addition, simultaneously with the experience of ecstasy, you also realize the reality of Self. You recognize your real nature and you know, "I am only bliss (*ānanda*) and consciousness (*cit*)."

And when you maintain that bliss through the grace of your master, then the force of *cit kuṇḍalinī* pierces *bhrūmadhya*, which is found between the eyebrows. At that point, at once and abruptly, you breathe out. Here, you breathe out and not in and you do so only once. Once you breathe out, your breathing is once again stopped. Then *cit kuṇḍalinī* rises from *bhrūmadhya* to *brahmarandhra*, which is found at the top of the skull. You experience the rising flow of *cit kuṇḍalinī* as filling the

---

the ordinary course of breathing. When *iḍā* is present, then you breathe more through the right nostril. When *piṅgalā* is there, then you breathe more through the left nostril. When *suṣumnā* is present then you breathe equally through both nostrils. *Iḍā*, *piṅgalā*, and *suṣumnā* have nothing to do with *kuṇḍalinī*.

3 sparśo yadvat pipīlikā

whole channel from *mūlādhāra* to *brahmarandhra*. Here again you abruptly breathe out and your eyes are open. This lasts for only a moment and then you are again inside, without breathing, experiencing the rise of *kuṇḍalinī*. Then again you breathe out and again your eyes are open and for a moment you feel that the outside world is full of ecstasy and bliss. This happens again and again. One moment you are inside experiencing the bliss of the rise of *cit kuṇḍalinī* and then the next moment you breathe out and your eyes are open and you are experiencing the world filled with ecstasy. This process of coming out and remaining in continues and each time it occurs, it is filled with more and more ecstasy. This process is called *krama mudrā*.

When you are established in the process of *krama mudrā*, then you experience that ecstasy in action. When you eat, you are in that bliss. When you talk, you are in that bliss. When you walk, you are in that bliss. Whatever you do, you remain in that Universal state. This is the state of *jīvanmukti*, liberated in life. This state is experienced not by ordinary *yogins*, but only by great *yogins*. This is the real state of *cit kuṇḍalinī*.

In the actual rise of *cit kuṇḍalinī,* you will only get a glimpse of it and then come out. The full rise of *cit kuṇḍalinī* takes place only by the grace of your master and by the grace of your own strength of awareness. The experience of establishing the full rise of *cit kuṇḍalinī* through the process of *krama mudrā* can take place in one day, one life, or one hundred lifetimes.

Prāṇa kuṇḍalinī also comes about through the process of centering. *Prāṇa kuṇḍalinī*, however, is only experienced by those *yogins* who, along with their attachment to spirituality, also have attachments to worldly pleasures. If your desire and attachment is only for spirituality, then *cit kuṇḍalinī* takes place. Whether you experience the rise of *kuṇḍalinī* as *cit kuṇḍalinī* or as *prāṇa kuṇḍalinī* depends on your attachments. If you have attachment for spirituality and also for worldly pleasures, then the rise of *kuṇḍalinī* takes place in the form of *prāṇa kuṇḍalinī*. If you do not have attachments for worldly pleasures and are only attached to spirituality, then the rise of *kuṇḍalinī* takes place in the form of *cit kuṇḍalinī*. There is nothing you can do to determine how the rise of *kuṇḍalinī* will take place. It rises in its own way, depending on your attachments.

Up to the point where your breath is sipped down in the central vein rushing to *mūlādhāra cakra* and through the momentary experience of the crawling sensation, the rise of *cit kuṇḍalinī* and the rise of *prāṇa kuṇḍalinī* are the same. In the rise of *prāṇa kuṇḍalinī*, however, when the crawling sensation is finished, then, in the state of *mūlādhāra*, there is a *cakra* (wheel)[4] and this *cakra* begins moving forcefully with great speed in a clockwise direction. At the same time, the *yogin* will also hear the sound of its movement.

After some time, that force rises twelve finger-spaces from *mūlādhāra cakra* to *nābhi cakra*, which is the *cakra* of the navel. When it reaches the navel, then the *cakra* of the navel also begins to move and you feel that simultaneously two wheels are in motion and you hear the sound of that movement. Here, as in *cit kuṇḍalinī*, the intensity of real love[5] blooms forth. It is so full of love and ecstasy that the experience of sexual bliss at the height of intercourse completely pales in comparison.

It is important for you to know that in the process of *prāṇa kuṇḍalinī*, you may not go beyond *mūlādhāra cakra* or beyond

4 In some *śāstras*, it is said that these *cakras* contain lotus petals. In Śaivism, these petals are not experienced nor are they recognized.

5 Love is the stuff of life. Without love you are not living. It is just as if you were dead. I am not speaking of sexual love; I mean real love. Real love exists in *kuṇḍalinī*.

nābhi cakra. You may only experience *mūlādhāra cakra* and then come out into ordinary life. Then again you will have to begin with your practice of centering. For the full experience of *prāṇa kuṇḍalinī*, whether you are a householder, married or unmarried, you have to give your full life to it.

From *nābhi cakra,* the force rises to *hṛit cakra*, which is the *cakra* of the heart, and which is experienced as being right in the center in between the two breasts. When the force reaches *hṛit cakra*, it also begins to move and you feel all three wheels spinning with great velocity, you hear their sound, and you even experience the spokes that comprise their wheels. From *hṛit cakra,* the force of breath rises up to *kaṇṭhacakra*, the *cakra* at the pit of the throat, and this *cakra* also begins to rotate at a very high speed. From *kaṇṭhacakra*, the force of breath reaches to *bhrūmadhya cakra*, the *cakra* found between the two eyebrows, and it also begins to rotate. With the movement of *bhrūmadhya cakra,* we have come to the end of the process of movement.

When the force of breath moves from *bhrūmadhya cakra*, rising to *sahasrāra cakra*, *sahasrāra cakra* does not begin rotating. It does not move; rather, it is pierced by great *yogins*. And this piercing does not always take place. Sometimes it is pierced and sometimes it is not, depending on whether or not you have attachment to worldly pleasures. This piercing will only take place when you do not have any attachment for worldly pleasures. And when you do pierce this *cakra*, then you become completely filled with bliss and enter into the process of *cit kuṇḍalinī*.

If you do not pierce this *cakra* then, you will only travel up to *bhrūmadhya cakra* and from *bhrūmadhya cakra,* you will come out and achieve *aṣṭasiddhiḥ*, the eight great yogic powers. These powers are *aṇimā*, *laghimā*, *mahimā*, *garimā*, *īśitvam*, *vaśitvam*, *prākāmyam*, and *kāmāvasayitvam-vyāpti*.

Aṇimā is the power of becoming invisible. *Laghimā* is the power to become so light that you can move through the air. *Mahimā* is the power to create and maintain, as Hanumān did, an enormous body. *Garimā* is the power to add weight to your body so that you become immovable. *Īśitvam* is the power to have control over the cosmos, e.g., you have the power to make it rain or to make the sun shine. *Vaśitvam* is the power to make yourself attractive so that everyone wants to be with you. *Prākāmyam* is the power to have control over your own bodily system. *Prākāmyam* enables you to create hunger where there is none, or if you are hungry, to eliminate your feelings of hunger. The eighth power is *vyāpti,* which is the power to pervade the whole universe. This power enables you to know what is occurring anywhere in the universe.

The danger inherent in these powers lies in the fact that when you have and use them then by and by, you will be deprived of some portion of your spirituality. This occurs because, due to the charm of these powers, you become ever more devoted to worldly pleasures.

In Kashmir Śaivism, there is a second way that *prāṇa kuṇḍalinī* may rise. Just through bad luck, it sometimes rises in reverse. In the reverse rise of *prāṇa kuṇḍalinī*, when the breath is sipped down in the central vein and reaches *mūlādhāra cakra,* you will find that *mūlādhāra cakra* is not moving. Instead, *bhrūmadhya cakra* is moving. In fact, what has happened is that the breath has crossed all of the *cakras*, beginning with *mūlādhāra cakra* and has reached and penetrated *bhrūmadhya cakra*, which then begins to move. The force of the breath penetrates *kaṇṭha cakra* and it begins to move. Then the force of the breath moves to the heart, then to the navel, and finally reaches *mūlādhāra cakra* and all these *cakras* are in movement. Then you come out. The process of the reverse rise of *kuṇḍalinī* is completed. This is the incorrect process of *prāṇa kuṇḍalinī*. It is called *piśācāveśaḥ*, which means "trance of ghosts."[6] It is a fruitless and valueless process. It only happens when your master is not on good terms with you or is angry with you. He puts you in this process. In this reverse process, you do not go anywhere or achieve anything. In fact, it leads you from right to wrong.

---

6 viṣayeṣveva saṁlīnānadho'dhaḥ pātayantyaṇūn |
rūdrāṇūnyāḥ samāliṅgya ghorataryo'parāḥ smṛitāḥ

"These energies, which are the *ghoratarī* energies of Rudra, carry the individual downward by increasingly entangling him in the joy of the senses."

Mālinī Vijaya Tantra: III;31

Chapter Eighteen

Variations in the Rise of *Prāṇa Kuṇḍalinī*

There are variations in the rise of *prāṇa kuṇḍalinī* from *mūlādhāra cakra,* depending on the desires and longings of the aspirant. When a *yogin* has an intense longing for achieving the recognition of Supreme "I" through the *mantra* "*ahaṁ*" (I am), then, because of this desire and longing, his breath becomes full of bliss, joy, and ecstasy. Automatically, this blissful force of breath penetrates *mūlādhāra cakra* in the form of this *mantra*. He feels simultaneously that he is the existence of, and one with, this rise of *kuṇḍalinī*. This sensation then moves and rises with the penetrating force of blissful breath from *mūlādhāra cakra* and penetrates *nābhi cakra*, which is found in the navel. From the navel it penetrates *hṛit cakra*, which is found in the heart, and from the heart it penetrates *kaṇṭha cakra*, which is found in the throat. And finally, from the throat it penetrates *bhrūmadhya cakra*, which is found between the eyebrows. This particular kind of penetration, brought about by the force of the *mantra ahaṁ*, "I am," is called *mantravedha* in our Śaivism.

A different type of rising takes place when a *yogin* desires to uplift people. This *yogin* possesses this particular intensity of desire and feels that he is doing his practice for the benefit of mankind. He does not want to help himself, he wants to help others. For him, the rise of *prāṇa kuṇḍalinī* begins with the blissful force of breath touching *mūlādhāra cakra,* which then begins to move. Simultaneously the blissful force of breath is transformed into *nāda*. Here, *nāda* means "I am meant for the upliftment of mankind." Literally, the word *nāda* means "sound." It is called *nāda* because this *yogin* wants to explain the Universal Reality to others. This sensation of *nāda* continues as *prāṇa kuṇḍalinī* rises to penetrate the navel, then the heart, then the throat, and finally, the eyebrows. This particular type of penetration is called *nādavedha.*

The next variation in the rise of *prāṇa kuṇḍalinī* takes place when a *yogin* is attached to ease, comfort, happiness, and joy. He wants peace of mind and nothing else. In this case, when the blissful force of breath in the form of *prāṇa kuṇḍalinī* penetrates *mūlādhāra cakra* and then rises to penetrate the navel, heart, throat, and eyebrows, it is transformed into a fountain of semen. He feels that it is a fountain of semen which is rising from *mūlādhāra cakra* to *brahmarandhra* and spreading throughout his body. It rises with tremendous force, just like a fountain. How joyful and happy he becomes! Sexual joy is nothing in comparison. Due to the intensity of joy inherent in this particular rise of *prāṇa kuṇḍalinī,* he at once loses all taste for worldly pleasures. This kind of penetration is called *binduvedha.*

Another variation in the rise of *prāṇa kuṇḍalinī* takes place when a *yogin* has the desire to become strong and to maintain his strength. He would like to maintain himself in perfect condition. He would like to be able to teach others concerning his internal feelings without experiencing any fatigue. In this person, when the blissful force of breath penetrates *mūlādhāra cakra* and then rises to penetrate the navel, heart, throat, and eyebrows, it rises in the form of an ant. This is because the blissful force of breath is transformed into energy. This is the rise of energy in *prāṇa kuṇḍalinī*. He feels that energy is being developed and that he is becoming the embodiment of energy. This particular type of penetration in *prāṇa kuṇḍalinī* is called *śāktavedha*.

The fifth variation in the rise of *prāṇa kuṇḍalinī* takes place when a *yogin* has the impression that the form and reality of *kuṇḍalinī* is actually serpent power. When the *yogin* has this impression, then the rise of that blissful force of breath in the form of *prāṇa kuṇḍalinī* arises in the form of a cobra. He actually experiences that it is a cobra which is rising, with its tail remaining in and touching *mūlādhāra cakra* and its body stretching to penetrate all of the *cakras* up to and including *brahmarandhra*. This kind of penetration is called *bhujaṅgavedha*.

The sixth and last variation in the rise of *prāṇa kuṇḍalinī* takes place when the *yogin* acquires, in the course of his practice, the desire to secretly initiate a few of his disciples without anyone knowing. For this *yogin*, when the blissful force of breath penetrates *mūlādhāra cakra* and rises from *mūlādhāra cakra* to penetrate the navel, heart, throat, and eyebrows, it rises in the form of the buzzing of a black bee. He experiences the sound of a black bee and he also experiences intense bliss associated with this rise. This type of penetration is called *bhramaravedha*.

Of these six variations of penetration which take place in the rise of *prāṇa kuṇḍalinī*, I would appreciate experiencing only two of them, *mantravedha* and *binduvedha*. I would give everything for the experience of these two. Whether or not you experience a particular kind of penetration, however, is out of your hands. It is automatically determined by your deepest desires and longings.

Chapter Nineteen

The Schools of Kashmir Śaivism

Kashmir Śaivism is known as the Pure Trika System. The word *trika* means "the threefold science of man and his world." In the idea of *trika,* there are three energies: *parā* (supreme), *aparā* (lowest), and *parāparā* (combination of the lowest and the highest). These three primary energies represent the threefold activities of the world. In the thought of Trika, therefore, it is admitted that this whole universe and every action in it, whether spiritual, physical, or worldly, is existing in these three energies.

The Trika Philosophy is meant for any human being without restriction of caste, creed, or color. Its purpose is to enable you to rise from individuality to universality. The Trika System is comprised of four sub systems, the Pratyabhijñā system, the Kula system, the Krama system, and the Spanda system. These four systems, which form the one thought of the Trika system, all accept, and are based on, the same scriptures. These scriptures, which in Śaivism are called *āgamas,* are the ninety-two *āgamas* of Śaivism, the monistic *Bhairava Śāstras* which are supreme (*parā*) and which are sixty four in number; the mono-dualistic *Rūdra Śāstras* which are medium (*parā-*

parā) and which are eighteen in number; and the dualistic *Śiva Śāstras* which are inferior (*aparā*) and which are ten in number.

Pratyabhijñā System

The word *pratyabhijñā* means "to spontaneously once again recognize and realize your Self." Here you have only to realize, you do not have to practice. There are no *upāyas* (means) in the Pratyabhijñā system. You must simply recognize who you are.

Wherever you are, whether you are at the level of Supreme Being, at the level of *yoga*, or at that level which is disgusting, you can recognize your own Nature then and there without moving anywhere or doing anything. For example, take the case of a bride and groom. The woman has not seen her husband-to-be and craves to see him. Concerning him she has only heard praise and glory but she has not actually met him. Suppose this girl and her future husband happen by chance to go separately on the same pilgrimage. When they arrive at the place of pilgrimage, they meet. The girl, however, does not feel any importance in this man because she does not know him to be her future husband. Yet her future husband and this man are the same person. Later, when a friend introduces her to him, telling her that this is the man who is to be her husband, then she is filled with happiness, pleasure, and ecstasy. She realizes that this is the same man she had seen before.[1] In the same way, reality dawns in the Pratyabhijñā system. In whichever level you are situated, do not mind. The moment recognition

1 taistairapyupayācitairupanata-
stamvyāḥ sthito'pyāntike
kānto lokasamāna evam-
aparijñāto na rantuṁ yatha |

(*pratyabhijñāna*) dawns, not only do you instantaneously become divine, but you also realize that you were already divine. At that moment, you realize that you were already the Lord but did not know it because you had misunderstood yourself.

In the Pratyabhijñā philosophy, it is your master who tells you that you are the same person for whom you are longing and who teaches you to reach the goal there and then without adopting any means. This teaching, therefore, is situated chiefly in *anupāya*, which is that means where there are no means at all. It is the recognition that there was nothing to be done and nowhere to go. Here, there is no practice, no concentration, no meditation. By the grace of your master you realize it and you are there.

The Pratyabhijñā System flourished in the beginning of *Kali yuga*. As time passed, however, it became veiled due to misunderstanding. It wasn't until the end of the eighth century A.D. that the great master Somānanda reintroduced the Pratyabhijñā System in Kashmir. Somānanda's disciple was Utpaladeva, and his disciple was Lakṣmaṇagupta, and his disciple was the very great Abhinavagupta.

Kula System

The Kula System teaches you how you can live in *caitanya* (Universal Consciousness), the real nature of yourself, in both the ascending and the descending act. While you rise from the

---

lokasyaiṣa tathānavekṣitaguṇaḥ
svātmāpi viśveśvaro
naivālaṁ nijavaibhavāya
tadiyaṁ tatpratyabhijñoditā ||
Īśvarapratyabhijñā Kārikā: IV;2

lowest to the highest state, you realize your nature, and while you descend from the highest to the lowest state, you also realize your nature. In the Kula System, there is no break in the realization of your own nature either in the highest or in the lowest circle. This system, therefore, teaches you how you can live in totality.[2] In fact, the word *kula* means "totality."

In the practice of the Kula System, you have to realize the totality of the universe in one particle. Take one particle of anything which exists in this world. In that one particle there is to be realized the totality of the whole universe. The totality of energy is found in one particle. Everything is full of one thing and one thing is full of all things.[3]

The difference between the Pratyabhijñā System and the Kula System is only that the Pratyabhijñā System teaches you how to realize your own nature in one place and exist there, reside there, while the Kula System teaches you how you can rise from the lowest degree to the highest degree, and all the while experience the nature of your Self on the same level and state. Śiva, which is realized in *pṛithvī tattva,* is the same level, the same reality of Śiva which is realized in *śiva tattva*. Here, there is complete realization in every act of the world.

The Kula System was introduced in Kashmir in the beginning of the 5th century A.D. by Śṛīmacchandanātha. Later, in

2 Totality does not mean where there is only knowledge and not ignorance or where there is only ignorance and not knowledge. Totality is that state where knowledge and ignorance exist together; when there is knowledge, there is ignorance and when there is ignorance, there is knowledge. Both knowledge and ignorance are digested in the totality; nothing is excluded.

3 ekaikatrāpi tattve'pi ṣaṭtriṁśattattvarūpatā

"In any one element, you will find all of the thirty-six elements."

the 9th century, because its teachings had become distorted, it was reintroduced by Sumatinātha. In the line of masters that followed from Sumatinātha, Somanātha was his disciple. Śambhunātha was the disciple of Somanātha, and the great Abhinavagupta was the disciple of Śambhunātha.

Krama System

The Krama System does not recognize the ways of either the Pratyabhijñā System or of the Kula System. In the Krama System, you must rise in succession, step by step. This system teaches that step-by-step realization makes your realization firm. As the Krama System is concerned with successive realization, it is primarily concerned with space and time because where there is succession, there you find the existence of space and time. In both the Pratyabhijñā System and the Kula System, you are beyond space and time. In the Krama System, it is in the end, not in its process, that you are beyond time and space because it also carries you to that timeless and spaceless state.

The Krama System is primarily attributed to *śāktopāya* and to the twelve *kālīs*. The twelve *kālīs* are said to be the twelve movements of any one cognition. For example, if you look at any object, such as a pot, the sensation travels from your thought to the place of the pot and then returns again from the place of the pot to your thought, giving you the sensation whereby you realize this pot. You do not realize this pot at the place of the pot, you realize this pot in your mind. Your perception has moved from inside to the pot and then returned again from the pot to your thought. And these movements are distributed in twelve ways, as the twelve *kālīs* in the Krama System.

The rise of *prāṇa kuṇḍalinī* is also described in the Krama System because in *prāṇa kuṇḍalinī,* you rise from one *cakra* to another, from one state to another state. As this is a successive process, it is found in the Krama System.

Although the Krama System existed in the beginning of *Kali yuga*, having been introduced by the sage Durvāsā, it was reintroduced at the end of the 7th century A.D. in Kashmir by the sage Erakanātha, who was also known as Śivānandanātha. Śivānandanātha had only three chief disciples which he initiated into the Krama System. Because in this system predominance is given only to *śakti*,[4] all three were females. Their names were Keyūravatī, Madanikā, and Kalyāṇikā. They were quite prominent and were completely informed in the Krama System. Afterwards, these ladies also initiated disciples, which were both male and female.

Spanda System

The fourth system which comprises the Trika philosophy is called the Spanda System. The word *spanda* means "movement." The Spanda School recognizes that nothing can exist without movement. Where there is movement, there is life and where there is no movement, that is lifelessness. They realize that there is movement in wakefulness, dreaming, deep sleep, and *turya*. Though some thinkers argue that there is no movement in deep sleep, the philosophers of the Spanda System realize that nothing can exist without movement.

The teachings of the Spanda System, which is an important practical system, are found embodied in the "*Vijñāna Bhairava Tantra*," the "*Svacchanda Tantra*," and in the 6th chapter of the "*Tantrāloka*."

4 In this system you will find *Tantras* where Pārvatī initiates Śiva and Śiva becomes the disciple.

The Spanda System was introduced in Kashmir by the great sage Vasuguptanātha in the beginning of the 8th century A.D. Vasuguptanātha is the author of both the "*Śiva Sūtras*" and the "*Spanda Kārikās.*"[5] The disciple of Vasuguptanātha was Kallaṭa.

---

5 Some teachers think that the "Spanda Kārikās" were not composed by Vasuguptanātha but rather by his disciple Kallaṭa. This theory, however, is absolutely incorrect.

The Author: Swami Lakshmanjoo

Swami Lakshmanjoo was born in Srinagar, Kashmir on May 9, 1907. He was the last and the greatest of the saints and masters of the tradition of Kashmir Shaivism. He had a deep understanding of the philosophy and practices of Kashmir Shaivism. He was like a splendid and rare jewel. He spent his whole life, beginning when he was a small boy, studying and practicing the teachings of this tradition and in so doing has, because of his intellectual power and the strength of his awareness, realized both spiritually and intellectually the reality of its thought.

Being born with a photographic memory learning was always easy. In addition to complete knowledge of Kashmir Shaivism, he had a wide-ranging knowledge of the traditional religious and philosophical texts of India. When translating or teaching he would freely draw on other texts to clarify, expand and substantiate his teaching. He could recall a text by simply remembering the first few words of the verse. In time his reputation as a learned philosopher and spiritual adept spread. Spiritual leaders and scholars journeyed from all over the world to receive his blessing and to ask him questions about various aspects of Kashmir Shaiva philosophy. He gained renown as a devotee of Lord Shiva and as a master of the non dual tradition of Kashmir Shaivism.

Throughout his life Swami Lakshmanjoo taught his disciples and devotees the ways of devotion and awareness. He shunned fame and recognition and did not seek his own glory. He knew Kashmir Shaivism was a most precious jewel and that by God's grace, those who desired to learn would be attracted to it. His earnest wish was that it be preserved and made available to all who desired to know it.

On September 27, 1991 Swami Lakshmanjoo attained the great liberation and left his physical body.

Lakshmanjoo ACADEMY

The teachings of Swami Lakshmanjoo are a response to the urgent need of our time: the transformation of consciousness and the evolution of a more enlightened humanity.

The Universal Shaiva Fellowship and its educational branch, The Lakshmanjoo Academy, a fully accredited non-profit organization, was established under Swamij's direct inspiration, for the purpose of realizing Swamiji's vision of making Kashmir Shaivism available to the whole world. It was Swamiji's wish that his teachings be made available without the restriction of caste, creed or color. The Universal Shaiva Fellowship and the Lakshmanjoo Academy have preserved Swamiji's original teachings and are progressively making these teachings available in book, audio and video formats.

This knowledge is extremely valuable and uplifting for all of humankind. It offers humanity a clear and certain vision in a time of uncertainty. It shows us the way home and gives us the means for its attainment.

For information on Kashmir Shaivism or to support the work of The Universal Shaiva Fellowship and the Lakshmanjoo Academy and its profound consciousness work,

visit the Lakshmanjoo Academy website or

email us at info@LakshmanjooAcademy.org.

www.LakshmanjooAcademy.org

Instructions to download audio files

1. Open this link to download the free audio . . .
   https://www.universalshaivafellowship.org/Secret

   It will **direct** you to "**Kashmir Shaivism, The Secret Supreme - Audio**".

2. Select "**Add to basket "** which will send you to the next page.

3. Copy "**Secret"** into the "**Add Gift Certificate or Coupon"** box

4. Click "**Checkout**" and fill in your details to process the free downloads.

If you have any difficulties please contact us at:
www.LakshmanjooAcademy.org/contact

Printed in Great Britain
by Amazon

28185730R00101